Simon Vibert offers a fresh and very he
twelve effective modern-day preachers a
improve the standards in our churches. I

REV. DR. MICHAEL GREEN, Oxford Centre for C

Excellence in Preaching is down-to-earth, challenging and full of gems. In surveying different preachers, and what we learn from them, Simon Vibert cuts across the party lines of evangelicalism and encourages all who preach to think what it is that makes people listen. Set on the foundation and conviction of biblically persuasive, Christ-focused and urgently applied preaching, with the Lord Jesus as our model, we find ourselves sitting at the feet of those whom God has raised up as preachers in this generation. This book will not allow anyone to get away with complacent preaching and is, therefore, both a challenge and an encouragement to all who love the Lord, love his Word, and long for his people to grow.

REV. SIMON AUSTEN, vicar of St. John's Houghton and St. Peter's Kingmoor, Carlisle

With great insight and even-handedness, Simon Vibert looks at twelve well-known, modern-day preachers, culling from their sermons the one thing that they do best. By the time he finishes his survey of the twelve communicators, Vibert has fashioned a compelling case for what great biblical preaching looks like.

We all long for more powerful, engaging and effective preaching in our churches. This book goes a long way in helping us to reach that goal. As someone who has been preaching for almost seventeen years, I discovered that my views on preaching were both confirmed and challenged by reflecting on *Excellence in Preaching*. I am grateful that Simon took the time to write this book.

JIM BELCHER, author of *Deep Church,* and associate professor of practical theology, Knox Theological Seminary

This book will be an encouragement to all who preach the Word, week-in and week-out. In examining the work of twelve very different but well-known preachers, Dr. Vibert encourages us to listen to and to learn from each of them. *Excellence in Preaching* serves to remind us that there is no "perfect sermon," but that all who preach have much to learn from others. This book will surely encourage many to renew their passion for the preaching of God's Word.

REV. DR. PAUL GARDNER, senior pastor of Christchurch, Atlanta

An inspiring, accessible and engaging book for preachers, at whatever stage in their preaching ministry. Simon Vibert challenges us to take the preaching of the Word of God seriously in an innovative manner. The way in which such a variety of excellent preachers has been presented in this book, with their particular strengths highlighted, makes it easy for us to learn from them. The examples of good preachers, in all their diversity, challenge us to review how we preach. We are encouraged not to try to be like clones, but instead develop our own style of good preaching.

A must-read for anyone who takes preaching seriously.

REV. CLARE HENDRY, minister for pastoral care, St. James Church, Muswell Hill, London, and formerly on the staff at Oak Hill Theological College

Many things will help raise the standard of preaching around the world, but one of the most significant—and underrated—is the need for good models. Simon Vibert provides compelling examples of what constitutes good preaching, not that we emulate superstars, but that we learn from the dynamic interplay of the Word, the Spirit, the congregation and the rich variety of human personality. This is an illuminating read for preachers and listeners alike, and I warmly commend it.

JONATHAN LAMB, director, Langham Preaching, Langham Partnership International; chair, Keswick Convention

Simon Vibert serves us well in this book. First, he rediscovers a passion and vision for preaching the Bible, at a time when some have recommended doing away with preaching. Secondly, his survey of what good preachers do well gives us some timely advice and suggestions. Thirdly, he models a willingness to learn from other preachers—and he's been a preacher for many years himself, but still sees the need to listen, learn and work at his preaching!

For these reasons and more, I hope young and experienced preachers alike will read this book in order to gain a passion and vision for preaching the Bible, do their task well and be humble learners and listeners themselves.

REV. DR. GAVIN MCGRATH, senior associate minister, Dundonald Church, London

The most effective preachers know how much they need throughout their lives to continue learning to preach—and one of their best sources of ongoing training is through studying other preachers. Here are a dozen preachers of excellence from whom all of us can learn who have the privilege and responsibility to teach others.

PAUL PERKIN, vicar, St. Marks, Battersea Rise, London

This is an imaginative and encouraging book, demonstrating how the best of the best of preachers actually [preach]. Fresh, stimulating and constantly challenging, it made me want to start preparing a sermon immediately! I can't imagine any preacher not being inspired to pick up the task with new courage, and at the same time to give thanks for the privilege.

THE RT. REV. JOHN PRITCHARD, bishop of Oxford

EXCELLENCE IN PREACHING

Studying the Craft of Leading Preachers

Simon Vibert

IVP Books

An imprint of InterVarsity Press
Downers Grove, Illinois

InterVarsity Press
P.O. Box 1400, Downers Grove, IL 60515-1426
Internet: www.ivpress.com
E-mail: email@ivpress.com

InterVarsity Press® is the book-publishing division of InterVarsity Christian Fellowship/USA®, a
movement of students and faculty active on campus at hundreds of universities, colleges and schools
of nursing in the United States of America, and a member movement of the International Fellowship
of Evangelical Students. For information about local and regional activities, write Public Relations
Dept., InterVarsity Christian Fellowship/USA, 6400 Schroeder Rd., P.O. Box 7895, Madison, WI
53707-7895, or visit the IVCF website at <www.intervarsity.org>.

All Scripture quotations, unless otherwise indicated, are taken from the Holy Bible, New
International Version®. NIV®. Copyright ©1973, 1978, 1984 by International Bible Society. Used
by permission of Hodder and Stoughton Ltd. All rights reserved. "NIV" is a registered trademark of
International Bible Society. UK trademark number 1448790. Distributed in North America by
permission of Zondervan Publishing House.

While all stories in this book are true, some names and identifying information in this book have
been changed to protect the privacy of the individuals involved.

Cover design: Cindy Kiple
Interior design: Beth Hagenberg
Images: John Piper: Bethlehem Baptist Church
        Nicky Gumbel: HTB /Alpha International, London, England
        John Ortberg: Jeanne dePolo Photography, Redwood City, CA
        Tim Keller: Redeemer Presbyterian Church

ISBN 978-0-8308-3815-8

Printed in the United States of America ∞

Library of Congress Cataloging-in-Publication Data

A catalog record for this book is available from the Library of Congress.

| P | 18 | 17 | 16 | 15 | 14 | 13 | 12 | 11 | 10 | 9 | 8 | 7 | 6 | 5 | 4 | 3 | 2 | 1 |
| Y | 26 | 25 | 24 | 23 | 22 | 21 | 20 | 19 | 18 | 17 | 16 | 15 | 14 | 13 | 12 | 11 |

❖

*To my colleagues and students at
Wycliffe Hall who give me much hope for
the future of preaching.*

CONTENTS

PREFACE

❖

Whenever a new book appears, readers have a right to ask what justifies its existence. Additionally, in this case, here is a book on preaching—words about words! And has not everything already been said that needs to be said about preaching?

So why this book? What's new in the contemporary preaching scene is this: freely available mass communication. Accordingly, this book seeks to assist preachers and hearers alike to make the very most of the worldwide reach of today's pulpit ministry.

One result of the World Wide Web is that it has greatly enhanced our ability to lend our ears to preachers beyond our local church pastor. However, this new media also raises some important questions about preaching and preachers in a worldwide context.

I don't intend to offer tips on the use of the mass media, particularly the (aptly named) "World Wide Web." Nor do I want to evaluate the Internet itself. My hope is to help today's church to make the very best use of the global and local preaching market. In other words, with a click of the mouse I may hear John Piper, Mark Driscoll, Tim Keller, Vaughan Roberts and countless other good preachers, but how can I do that profitably?

Listening to such preachers[1] is a veritable feast. I want to consider what it is that they do well, and why it is that people want to listen to them. Along the way I also want to ask: what does their Internet ministry have to do with the local church, or my pastor, or your preaching? Or more pointedly, is it possible to learn from the best preachers without devaluing the rather more ordinary week-in, week-out preaching of the local church?

I passionately believe that the answer to this last question is yes. We need wisdom to see the immense value in the preaching of faithful local pastors intimately tending God's flock. The Internet will never replace them. So I believe that it is possible to make use of modern technology without becoming disillusioned with the more relational, more local church.

My sustenance as a Christian, throughout my late teens and early twenties, came mostly from hearing cassettes of Dick Lucas: recordings of twenty-minute sermons preached to a congregation at St. Helen's Bishopsgate in the city of London. Dick set the standard high and still he makes me want to preach in such a way that the Bible becomes crystal clear to the congregation. But he also did something else for me: his sermons nourished me and drove me back into my small local congregation to live with all the foibles and inadequacies of much of the preaching which was offered, and to a fresh appreciation of what it was to be related to one another in Christ.

The best preachers make you strive for Christlikeness and value the great things that God is doing in his church. I hope that you too can reach this conclusion as we carefully examine the twelve preachers I have selected.

Simon Vibert

INTRODUCTION

Preaching the Bible Way

Preaching is under threat. Yet it is rare for the modern Western preacher to be shouted down, locked up in prison or forbidden by law to preach (although this scenario is a reality in many parts of the world today). The threat is a much more insidious one than that.

The sad caricature of the sermon is that it is an empty or incomprehensible droning from a cleric who is "six feet above contradiction." This is amusingly portrayed by Rowan Atkinson in the comedy drama *Mr. Bean*. In a sketch which takes place in a dreary church service, Mr. Bean is doing everything he can to stay awake during a sermon, and all that can be heard in the background is the wordless drone of a preacher. Despite his best efforts, Mr. Bean is soon lulled to sleep. Believing the oft-quoted caricature of preaching as "a monstrous monologue by a moron to a mute" is, arguably, the biggest threat to modern preaching.

This book seeks to build up a composite picture of a model preacher by looking at those things which good preachers do well. What makes us want to listen to them in particular? Why is it that some preachers make the time fly by, leaving us wanting more, sensing that we have connected with the living God?

The modern-day preachers whom you will meet are very different in style and, sometimes, content. Each has his own gifts, foibles and flaws. The old adage that preaching is "truth through personality" is as much a truism today as it has ever been. And I have had to be selective. There are of course many other contemporary examples of outstanding preachers who do the things these twelve do! My selection of preachers, almost exclusively from the Western Hemisphere, is reflective of the kind of people who have influenced and shaped me (as well as many of my students), rather than being an attempt to provide a thorough critique of all good preaching around the world. These are preachers with whom I have either had personal contact or who, for me, exemplify a pertinent characteristic of preaching. They themselves would be the first to acknowledge that they have not necessarily reached the "Top Twelve."

Part of my research involved a survey of fellow preachers, theological college students and congregational members. I wanted to find out who their favorite preachers were and what it was that made people want to listen to them. I was not looking for an analytical assessment but rather hoping that my respondents would give me their gut instinct. Why did they listen to one particular preacher and not another?

The results of my survey enabled me to shape my list.[1] I have had to be selective, and indeed many preachers exemplify more than one characteristic of preaching. But this is my book, and I have highlighted only one aspect from each of them in order to create a composite picture. This list is therefore not intended to be exhaustive, which is why, as an additional online resource, there is also a website which is continually being updated with the profiles of several more good preachers.[2]

This book sets out to achieve three things:

First, I hope that it will be a resource for those who seek to prepare and deliver biblical, applicable and illustrated contemporary sermons. We have much to learn from those who "do it well."

Second, I hope that it will help congregations (or, increasingly, sermon surfers) to know what to look for in a good preacher or, perhaps, to realize why they connect so well with certain preachers.

Third, as I've said earlier, I hope it will help us to appreciate and weigh up the strengths and limitations of being able to listen to good preachers at the click of a mouse.

I hope I have not written hagiography. This is not intended to start a guru mentality or a cult following (a particular problem among sermon surfers today). What I do hope is that, as a result of reading this book, preachers and their listening congregations will have a better sense of why it is that some preachers connect hearers with God, inspiring, encouraging and motivating them to authentic Christian living, and enabling them to leave with a sense that through the preaching they have indeed met with the living Lord.

THE PRIORITIES OF PREACHING

I doubt that you will have read thus far without some convictions about the importance of preaching. For me, there are three priorities.

Preaching should be pervasively biblical. Speaking to the leaders from the Ephesian church, the apostle Paul states:

> You know that I have not hesitated to preach anything
> that would be helpful to you but have taught you publicly
> and from house to house. . . . I have not hesitated to pro-
> claim to you the whole will of God. (Acts 20:20, 27)

Paul claims that his preaching was thorough (it was in people's homes as well as in public) and comprehensive (he
preached the whole will of God). Such preachers labor at making the entire Bible known to the whole of the community in
which they minister. It is not primarily about stories, anecdotes
or observations on life. Good preachers bring God's Word alive
for today's world.

Preaching should be both Christ- and gospel-focused. Mark begins his Gospel by telling readers about the preacher of good
news, John the Baptist. John's message is all about Jesus Christ
(see Mark 1:1-2). This same message from the lips of Jesus is a
call to repentance and faith in the gospel (Mark 1:15).

The apostle Paul sums up his preaching to the Christians in
Corinth as being about Christ and his saving death:

> I resolved to know nothing while I was with you except
> Jesus Christ and him crucified. I came to you in weakness
> and fear, and with much trembling. My message and my
> preaching were not with wise and persuasive words, but
> with a demonstration of the Spirit's power, so that your
> faith might not rest on men's wisdom, but on God's power.
> (1 Corinthians 2:2-5)

What makes preaching uniquely Christian is that it is both inspired by, and also pervasively about, Jesus Christ. His name
will often be on the lips of the best of today's preachers.

Preaching should be urgent and applied. In his final letter to Timothy, Paul places the weight of responsibility for the future health of the church on preachers of the Word:

> In the presence of God and of Christ Jesus, who will judge the living and the dead, and in view of his appearing and his kingdom, I give you this charge: Preach the Word; be prepared in season and out of season; correct, rebuke and encourage—with great patience and careful instruction. For the time will come when men will not put up with sound doctrine. Instead, to suit their own desires, they will gather around them a great number of teachers to say what their itching ears want to hear. (2 Timothy 4:1-3)

Preachers are commissioned by God, the one who will judge all people, to be urgent, careful, faithful and meticulous in their preaching. Such preachers stand in marked contrast with those who preach only when it is convenient or when their message is popular or when it suits them. Holy boldness and urgency are greatly needed today (more on this later).

I have not said anything yet about the godliness of the preacher or about the accompanying work of God the Holy Spirit in and through the preaching process. We will look at both of these essential ingredients of true preaching in the final chapter.

Restricting myself for now to the preached sermon, this is how I summarize what I believe goes on in good biblical preaching: *preaching is a powerful, relationally based summons by God through his true and living Word.*

- It is powerful (God working through preaching).
- It is relational (between preacher and people).

- It is a summons (propositional and heralded).

- It is truth (persuasive).

- It is living (contemporary).

Sermon *content* is clearly very important. Others have already written passionately, expansively and clearly about what goes into a sermon, so this is not my focus here.[3] But it would be simplistic to assume that content and style are unrelated, or that the shape, length, delivery and form are not affected or driven by the content of the sermon. In fact, what lies very much at the heart of this book's motivation is my conviction that these factors all interrelate to make up good preaching. (More about this in the conclusion.)

Communication matters, and therefore words matter. The art of rhetoric has been of particular media interest since the election of President Barack Obama.[4] This is not unrelated to the interest in homiletics (the art of preaching), taught in many American seminaries. In recent years teachers of preaching in the United Kingdom have recognized that there is considerably more involved in preaching than understanding and teaching the meaning of the text. Of course, there is nothing new in this realization (see chap. 1 on the preaching of Jesus). Modern preachers can learn much from great biblical preachers, and they would also do well to study the likes of Plato, Aristotle, Cicero and Augustine to appreciate what makes for good communication.

DAILY BREAD AND SUMPTUOUS FEASTS

One respondent to my survey made a wise observation. He had selected one of the preachers in this book as a favorite. He did so because he occasionally goes on to that preacher's website to listen to his marvelous sermons. But my respondent also observed that for his ongoing spiritual sustenance, the less flashy but godly faithfulness of his local preacher feeds and nourishes him with biblical food, week in, week out.

This is an important point. Being fed from preaching is similar to being fed with, well, food! Most of us eat three main meals per day (with perhaps countless snacks in between!). What did you eat for lunch yesterday? Or for dinner the day before? Or for breakfast last Monday? It is very likely that you will not be able to remember.

Feeding on the Bible is rather like this. "Man does not live on bread alone but on every word that comes from the mouth of the LORD" (Deuteronomy 8:3). There is something routine and pedestrian about this process.

On the other hand, some meals stand out: that wonderful Chinese meal a few weeks ago, the Christmas turkey roast dinner, the barbecue with friends in the warm sunshine. These are not routine meals required to keep you alive, but meals which titillate your appetite, delight you with great taste and satisfy you deeply. So it is with some sermons: they are sumptuous feasts rather than simply daily bread.

I can vividly remember a sermon preached by Dick Lucas, who remains one of my favorite preachers. He took as his text John 3:16: "For God so loved the world that he gave his one and only Son, that whoever believes in him shall not perish but have eternal life."

Twenty-five years later I can still remember the way in which he began his sermon: "Our text today is the most famous verse in the Bible, but the problem is that we do not believe it." Well, that certainly got my attention! He went on to say that "people today do not believe that Jesus is God's one and only Son, and they do not believe that failure to believe in Jesus Christ will mean that they will forever perish."

For me, this sermon was a feast. I saw old truths in a new light and I heard the Bible speaking to me with real freshness and pertinent application. Old truths hit home. The ingredients were familiar, but the arrangement, delivery and flavor made me hungry for more!

We are about to see some marvelous and perhaps exceptional examples of preaching. I hope that they will inspire you to greater heights, and, if you are a preacher, to preach better and be more faithful in the preaching task. I hope too that these examples will incite a fresh appetite for God and his Word, which will lead us to pray afresh, along with Samuel, "Speak, for your servant is listening" (1 Samuel 3:10).

1

JESUS CHRIST THE PREACHER

Setting the Supreme Standard

The world is full of books about Jesus Christ. But ironically Jesus did not write any books. His first followers called him Rabbi. Friends and enemies alike recognized him as a great teacher (a term used more than forty times in the Gospels). As we read Jesus' sermons and parables, we should remember by contrast that the crowds first *heard* them. Preparing a book on the things that great preachers do well, I have regularly and perhaps inevitably asked myself: is it possible to *hear* Jesus the preacher?

Of course we know nothing of Jesus' tone of voice, his inflection or his cadence. There was no MP3 recorder to help us analyze his speaking. His worldwide reach succeeded long before the Internet. The abiding power of his speech is felt today by the force of his imagery, his succinct phraseology and his challenging incisiveness.

But Jesus was obviously a compelling speaker. It goes without out saying that he stands out as the unique preacher and, unlike every other preacher in this book, is flawless and perfect in his preaching. The Gospels record the audiences' reactions: "The large crowd listened to him with delight" (Mark 12:37). Crowds followed him, even when he sought to withdraw in private (e.g., Luke 4:42-44). Jesus was also aware of the fickleness and impulsiveness of the crowd, particularly when they looked for dramatic miracles rather than taking seriously the message he sought to preach.

We would also do well to remember that Jesus was around when the art of public speaking was a prized gift. From a Jewish point of view generational education was given through skilled oral instruction. Rabbis were expected to teach their followers, and this included the practice of reciting familiar forms of prayers, proverbs and prose. For example, the Mishnah—the Jewish oral law—communicated the oral traditions of the law in a form that encouraged recollection and rote learning. A rabbi was a skilled oral communicator.

What was true for the history of Jewish education was even more evident in the Greco-Roman world. Those skilled in rhetoric (Plato, Aristotle, Cicero and others) captivated audiences by their displays of wisdom and persuasion.

Born into an environment steeped in good public oratory, Jesus, we can be fairly sure, knew something about the "rules" of public speaking, and his audiences were familiar with listening. For sure, Jesus surprised his followers with earthy, counterintuitive teaching methods. But it is also true that some of the contemporary patterns of rhetoric are evident in Jesus' use of words and language.

As we consider Jesus as a preacher, it is important primarily to hear what he has to say. Throughout its two-thousand-year history the church has emphasized the need to listen to, and even more, to hear, the Word of God.[1] The public reading of Scripture and the preaching of the Word of God are major parts of Christian worship, communal and communicative acts.

It was the conviction of the apostles that through preaching the audience could engage with God. For example, in Romans 10:14-17 Paul asks:

> How, then, can they call on the one they have not believed in? And how can they believe in the one of whom they have not heard? And how can they hear without someone preaching to them? And how can they preach unless they are sent? As it is written, "How beautiful are the feet of those who bring good news!"
>
> But not all the Israelites accepted the good news. For Isaiah says, "Lord, who has believed our message?" Consequently, faith comes from hearing the message, and the message is heard through the word of Christ.

The apostle's conviction was that faith comes not by reading but by hearing. And it is a certain kind of hearing which is important, namely hearing Jesus' words with a conviction that we need to put them into practice (Matthew 7:24). See also Jesus' comment, "He who has ears, let him hear" (Matthew 11:15; 13:9, 43).

I wonder, then, if it is possible for us to sit at the feet of Jesus today? Can we too "hear the word of Christ"?

THE SERMON ON THE MOUNT

Jesus' best-known teaching is encapsulated in the Sermon on the Mount (Matthew 5–7). A similar sermon, sometimes called the "Sermon on the Plain," is recorded in Luke 6, which would seem to imply that the Gospel writers have included a selected summary of Jesus' teachings which he gave to more than one audience on different occasions.

Nevertheless, the Sermon on the Mount is written up as if it was one sermon. Modern readers may still feel as though they are in the crowd, listening to Jesus preaching timeless and persuasive words. We should still try to hear it as a sermon today.

Jesus' sermon contains some of the best known and most quoted pieces of moral and ethical wisdom of all time. Phrases like "an eye for an eye," "turn the other cheek," "love your neighbor," to name but a few, are included, along with a prayer which we can still recite today (usually in traditional language): "Our Father who art in heaven, hallowed be thy name . . ."

Audience. Jesus goes to a mountainous area (perhaps with deliberate echoes of the giving of the Ten Commandments by Moses on Mount Sinai?) in order to teach his disciples. From this vantage point it would have been possible for his voice to be carried across the hill and down the slopes to where the crowds had gathered.

His intended audience seems to have been primarily his own closest followers. (According to custom, teachers sat down in order to teach.) But Matthew also makes it plain that there are crowds present: in other words, a wider and more general audience listening in. One memorable feature of good communicators is, in fact, their ability to speak at multiple levels. In Jesus' case this enabled devoted followers to go deeper in their understanding of the faith, while at the same time, his speaking with such simple clarity allowed first-time hearers to access the content. The Sermon on the Mount is a model of this type of communication. Matthew concludes his record with these comments: "When Jesus had finished saying these things, the crowds were amazed at his teaching, because he taught as one who had authority, and not as their teachers of the law" (Matthew 7:28-29).

Theme and content. The content of the sermon, as recorded by Matthew in Greek, contains around two thousand words. If this was all that Jesus said on this occasion, it would have taken under half an hour to deliver. However, as we have already noted, it is likely that Matthew recorded edited highlights, collating them in such a way that the modern reader may get a flavor of the overall flow and theme.

Scholars note the strong resonance with key themes in more recent Old Testament writings. For some, Jesus is a preacher of wisdom similar to the ancient sage or proverbial writer. For them, Jesus is to be heard as the supremely wise one whose words need to be heeded and applied.

For others, Jesus' words should be heard as apocalyptic warning, foretelling the end times which are implicit in the announcement of the king's arrival. The emphasis is upon the urgency of living faithfully in his kingdom, particularly as empires crumble and fall. His followers should be aware that his kingdom has been announced and proclaimed, but it is not yet fully evident to all. They will need to live with that kind of tension.

Both of these themes may be evident in Jesus' sermon: wise sayings coupled with urgent appeal. "Teaching plus exhortation" marks out this genre of preaching. The uniting theme of the Sermon on the Mount is: what it means to be a true disciple of Jesus Christ. Jesus begins by spelling out the nature of true discipleship (positively and negatively: what it is and what it isn't), and follows this up with a challenge to be righteous in a way that exceeds the usual pattern of righteousness as taught by the Pharisees.

Structure. In terms of formal rhetoric, the sermon uses common Old Testament devices to give it shape.

The first is *inclusio,* or "bookends." Words and themes introduced at the beginning are repeated at the end in order to bring to the speech a sense of completeness. This enables the audience to grasp the theme clearly introduced at the beginning: "Blessed are . . ." (Matthew 5:3-11) and then return to a clear conclusion: "Therefore everyone who hears these words of mine and puts them into practice is like a wise man who built his house on the rock . . ." (Matthew 7:24). The blessed and wise person is the follower who heeds Jesus' words.

The second rhetorical device is known as the *chiasm.* Subject matter appears in a symmetrical or rhythmic pattern to help hearers to remember it. This may be demonstrated as follows:

A1—5:3-10. Beatitudes. Who the disciples are
  B1—5:11-16. The disciples' vocation
    C1—5:17-19. Conditions for implementing the vocation
      D1—5:20. Introduction of antithesis (framing material)
        E1—5:21-47. Antithesis. The overabundant righteousness
      D2—5:47-48. Conclusions of the antithesis (framing material)
      D3—6:1. Introduction to the next unit (framing material)
        E2—6:2-16. The overabundant righteousness
      D4—6:19-21. Conclusion of preceding unit (framing material)
    C2—6:22–7:12. Conditions for implementing the vocation
  B2—7:13-20. The disciples' vocation
A2—7:21-27. Who the disciples are[2]

Through the use of "bookends" and "symmetry," it becomes clear that the central theme of discipleship is skillfully introduced and illustrated, and poignantly applied to the crowds.

Manner. How did Jesus seek to persuade his audience,

hold their attention and communicate in a way which (to quote Cicero) "taught, delighted and moved" them? What evidence is there in Jesus' teaching that he showed any awareness of the ancient Greek, Roman or Jewish history of rhetoric? And how, if at all, should today's preachers seek to preach as Jesus preached?

Authority. There are a number of ways in which Jesus assumes authority. He says things such as "verily" or "truly I say" or "I tell you the truth" (the word is *amen*). He also makes assumptions about his right to judge who will and will not be in the kingdom, and this on the basis of their acknowledgment of his authority.[3]

When Jesus says, "You have heard that it was said. . . . But I tell you" throughout chapter 5, he is building up a strong contrast between his authoritative teaching and that of the scribes and Pharisees. His authority is based upon his own interpretation of God's law. Their teaching usually includes long lists of citations from other teachers of the law: "Rabbi so-and-so says thus . . ." Jesus by contrast says, "I tell you . . ." This must have made a powerful impact on his hearers. His words need no bolstering from others; he claims a right to interpret the law for himself.

So Jesus speaks authoritatively, proclaiming the kingdom. Rhetoricians seek to persuade through rational deduction, whereas Jesus makes assumptions about his right to speak definitively, fully anticipating a response of obedience.

Rhetorical techniques. Anaphora is a verbal technique which makes use of the same word to begin a series of sentences. (The word *anaphora* comes from the Greek word meaning "I repeat.") Winston Churchill skillfully and successfully employed this device when he said,

We shall not flag or fail. . . .

We shall go on to the end. We shall fight in France, we shall fight on the seas and oceans, we shall fight with growing confidence and growing strength in the air, we shall defend our island, whatever the cost may be.

We shall fight on the beaches, we shall fight on the landing grounds, we shall fight in the fields and in the streets, we shall fight in the hills; we shall never surrender.[4]

By repeating the phrase "Blessed are . . . " Jesus draws the audience toward a cumulative conclusion: this is what it means to be truly blessed.

Syllogism is a form of deductive reasoning leading to a certain conclusion, illustrated in this familiar example: *All humans are mortal* (major irrefutable premise), *I am a human* (minor premise), *therefore, I am mortal* (inescapable conclusion). In the Sermon on the Mount the conclusion, stated at the first, is: all who are my disciples—those who are in my kingdom—are blessed. Minor premise: the poor in spirit are blessed. Major premise: the poor are in my kingdom. The unusual conclusion of these premises is based upon the assumed authority Jesus exercises in judging who will and will not be his true disciple.[5]

Metaphor. The sermon is full of powerful metaphors. Jesus says, for example, "If your right eye causes you to sin, gouge it out. . . . And if your right hand causes you to sin, cut it off and throw it away" (Matthew 5:29-30). Some preachers of Jesus' sermon did actually interpret these words literally. The third-century preacher Origen of Alexander (c. 185–c. 254), literally did emasculate himself. However, Jesus' immediate hearers apparently did not react to Jesus' teaching in such an impulsive, exacting way. They understood the rhetorical force of his message and heard the drastic language as metaphorical rather than literal.

Rhetorical questions assume that the audience understands the direction in which the sermon is going and is therefore able to anticipate answers to questions. Here are examples:

• "Is not life more important than food, and the body more important than clothes?" (Matthew 6:25). This is a no-brainer—life and body are of course more important than food and clothes.

• "Are you not much more valuable than [the birds of the air]?" (Matthew 6:26). Well, yes, we do not send an ambulance to take a bird to the emergency room, but humans have a whole medical system in place to rescue ailing people.

• "Who of you by worrying can add a single hour to his life?" (Matthew 6:27). No one can of course. Indeed, worry might have the opposite effect.

• "Which of you, if his son asks for bread, will give him a stone? Or if he asks for a fish, will give him a snake?" (Matthew 7:9-10). Once again the audience immediately knows that, though they are not perfect, they would not treat their children in this way, which enables Jesus logically to conclude: Why then is it any different when you think about your perfect heavenly Father?

Exaggeration, humor and graphic illustration. Jesus' use of colorful and memorable language would have elicited evocative imagery in the minds of his hearers, which would have assisted their ability to recall the key points of his sermon. Such phrases include "Why do you look at the speck of sawdust in your brother's eye and pay no attention to the plank in your own eye?" (Matthew 7:3). Imagine staggering around with a plank protruding out of your eye, while delicately trying to remove a shaving from your brother's!

Proverb. We are familiar with English proverbs such as "A leopard cannot change its spots" and "Absolute power corrupts absolutely." Such pithy proverbial sayings feature in this sermon, for example:

> You are the salt of the earth. But if the salt loses its saltiness, how can it be made salty again? It is no longer good for anything, except to be thrown out and trampled by men.
>
> You are the light of the world. A city on a hill cannot be hidden. Neither do people light a lamp and put it under a bowl. Instead they put it on its stand, and it gives light to everyone in the house. In the same way, let your light shine before men, that they may see your good deeds and praise your Father in heaven. (Matthew 5:13-16)

This fits in with the long Jewish history of the use of *mashal*, including proverbs, pithy sayings and so forth.[6] It was a form of communication which Jesus adapted and used to great effect in the longer parables in the rest of the Gospel.

Parable. It is clear that Jesus' use of parable was a significant feature of his communication (see Matthew 13:34). Some reckon that as much as one third of Jesus' teaching ministry was in the form of parable. This device acted as a sifting mechanism in order that those in his kingdom would grow in knowledge and appreciation, while outsiders, on the other hand, would remain perplexed and distanced. Parables were not supposed to be equally comprehensible to everyone. Jesus explains the purpose of this kind of teaching:

> Though seeing, they do not see;
>> though hearing, they do not hear or understand.
>> (Matthew 13:13)

So Jesus used parables to reveal truth to friends while concealing truth from his enemies. Some features of parables appear in brief form in the Sermon on the Mount.[7]

Ethos (personality and charisma). Jesus' sermon could be described as "dialogical." This does not necessarily mean that he took questions from the audience but rather that he anticipated and engaged with what they were thinking, and challenged the presumed wisdom of the day.

The "I and you" formula which Jesus repeated engaged them in a didactic relationship. This also implied authority. Jesus sought to draw them in so they felt that they wanted to belong to the "you" crowd.

"I and you" have now been replaced by the more inclusive "we and our" language of modern communication. But the "I and you" formula can be used with powerful effect when the audience recognizes the strength of character, weight, authority or leadership of the speaker. For example, Martin Luther King Jr. repeatedly used the phrase *I say to you*, as when he said: "Now, *I say to you* today, my friends, even though we face the difficulties of today and tomorrow, I still have a dream." People heard the weight of what he was saying because of the force of his authority. Billy Graham's passionate catchphrase "the Bible says" was used to great effect in a similar way in his evangelistic preaching. The striking thing about the way Billy Graham spoke was that he staked his own reputation not upon his eloquence but upon the authority of God's Word.

Logos (logic). The use of logic has already been alluded to in the earlier section on syllogism. The central section of the Sermon on the Mount concerning Jesus' claim to fulfill the law is important to the overall logic of the sermon. In effect Jesus is saying: You might be tempted to think this (that I am here to abolish the law), but you must think this instead (I have not come to abolish but to fulfill it). This leads to the strong conclusion in Matthew 5:20 about their righteousness needing to exceed that of the Pharisees and teachers of the law.

It is also important to observe that Jesus uses counterintuitive logic. Who would ever say that it is the poor who are blessed? Or that it is the mourners who are comforted? His teaching is subversive. His kingdom will be brought in unexpectedly through means that are very different from those of other human kings. Such words demand a lot of his hearers.

Pathos (emotion). Jesus did not seek to sway the crowds through hype or sensation. However, his sermon contains strong emotional appeal, capturing their imaginations, resonating with their concerns and challenging them to feel, as well as act, differently. Specifically, he uses emotionally laden words such as *rejoice, be glad, hate, peace, love, forgive, reward, worry* and *righteousness*. Such words are intended to have an emotional effect upon them: to comfort, to disturb, to provoke, to challenge and to appeal.[8]

Movement. Any speech or sermon needs a beginning, a middle and an end. We have already noted that Jesus begins by outlining what true members of his kingdom look like (Matthew 5:1-12). This is true discipleship. Jesus concludes with exhortations to enter the kingdom of God (Matthew 7:13-27).

The sermon contains a strong antithetical appeal—that is, there is no middle ground for the crowd to stand upon. Yet at the same time the language is inclusive and engaging: "everyone," "whoever," "anyone," he says.

The impact was to leave the crowd "amazed." They were far from bored or uninterested. Here was a preacher who had authority, in marked contrast to the teachers of the law with whom they were familiar. He drew them in and he left them wanting more.

LESSONS FOR PREACHERS TODAY

- Don't be afraid to use rhetorical techniques. A homiletical theme (the big idea) concentrates attention on a single thread running through the entire sermon.[9] When preachers are trained in a formal theological college or seminary setting, they can be inclined to write sermons as one long piece of prose. This is a good discipline. However, it is also important to practice rhetorical techniques which lodge thoughts into people's minds through their ears. Learning to do this can be greatly helped by noticing what good preachers do well.

- Draw in the congregation through a dialogical approach. Jesus clearly showed resonance with his audience by anticipating their concerns and answering their unspoken questions.

- Speak with authority. Clearly our authority cannot be the same as Jesus' authority ("You have heard that it was said. . . . I tell you"). However, we may speak with his authority as we announce his kingdom and call men and women to repent and follow him in lifestyles that are reflective of the King's claim on our life. The preacher is a herald, an authoritative emissary of the King.

- Provoke questions. Beware of scripting your sermon in

such a way that you have done all of the congregation's thinking for them. They should go away from the sermon provoked to think through what has been preached, pondering the implications, asking more questions and hungry to return for more.

2

Be Aware of Cultural and
Philosophical Challenges to the Gospel

Tim Keller is a pastor in the Presbyterian Church of America. He trained at Gordon-Conwell Theological Seminary and gained a doctor of ministry at Westminster Seminary, where he also served as professor. He and his wife, Kathy, live in New York City and have three sons.

Tim's most significant work has been as a church planter in New York, "one of Manhattan's most vital congregations," according to *Christianity Today*, in an article examining the impressive growth of Redeemer Presbyterian Church, which began in 1989 with only fifteen people.[1] The current congregation of around five thousand is spread across three locations. In recent years Redeemer has hosted church-planting conferences and trained hundreds of pastors from around the world seeking to transpose some of Redeemer's planting practice into their local context.

Tim's sermons contain humor, but this is not mere entertainment. His style is not flamboyant, nor is he a particularly energetic or showy preacher. His preaching demands your attention, and his sermons require concentration. But what makes Tim popular is that his preaching is so persuasive and engaging. He tackles difficult questions and leaves the congregation with a sense that those questions have profound, logical answers.

Both Tim Keller and John Piper (see chap. 3) are known as much for their writings as for their preaching. For this reason it might be helpful to orientate our thoughts on their preaching around some major themes, in addition to examining one particular sermon.

As a student in the doctor of ministry program at Reformed Theological Seminary in Orlando, I first heard Tim teach alongside the late Ed Clowney. The classes were titled "Preaching Christ in a Postmodern World."

Two things about those classes made a lasting impression on me. The first was the insight that all true Christian preaching had to be Christ-centered, whichever part of the Bible was turned to on any given Sunday. The unfolding of the story of God's rescue mission, climaxing in his sending Christ as sin-bearer on the cross, is the big story and plot line of the whole Bible. This is an important hermeneutical key to Tim's preaching.

The second insight (which Tim attributes to the key influence of Richard F. Lovelace in *Dynamics of Spiritual Life*, and before him to Martin Luther) is that the greatest need for the non-Christian and the Christian alike is the gospel.[2] For in the gospel my greatest need is both exposed and met in Christ. The gospel is necessary, not only for my justification but also for my sanctification. This essential Christian truth, which Tim claims lies at the heart of Martin Luther's message, cuts through the errors of both the legalist and the licentious, the "older" and the "younger brother" of Luke 15.[3]

The Reformation cry was the Latin phrase: *simul justus et peccator, totus totus* (simultaneously justified and sinner, totally justified and totally sinner). For Martin Luther this was one of the ways succinctly to articulate the very core of the gospel. Tim repeatedly phrases the same theme in his sermons: the gospel tells me that I am far worse, more flawed and more sinful than I imagine, and yet, simultaneously, I am more loved and accepted by God than I ever dared hope.

This critical insight enables Tim to preach to Christian and non-Christian alike, for both need the gospel. Emerging from these foundational themes are some central features, in particular the necessity of evangelism and social action going hand in hand, and this is not only regularly emphasized in preaching but also is the theme of a book.[4] At Redeemer Church they seek to "renew the city socially, spiritually and culturally."

The foundational themes are encapsulated in the church's vision for the future, which includes long-term community development, day care and church planting in New York City, transforming poor communities into prospering mixed-income neighborhoods. The vision involves the multiplication of churches, and resourcing them in faith and work, social justice, evangelism and community building. Redeemer Church seeks to encourage other churches to become gospel-based resources, designed to change hearts and form new communities of believing individuals, united in serving their cities with the love and hope of Christ.[5]

Tim has written several books, the most notable of which is *The Reason for God*. In it he articulates a rational case for belief in God. Many have commented, though, that Tim's primary gifts are the spoken ones: clarity of thought articulated in engaging and winsome persuasiveness. Hence Lisa Miller, in a

Newsweek article, "The Smart Shepherd," comments on *The Reason for God:* "The book is demanding, but ultimately it disappoints because its pages lack the charisma and conviction so evident in the man."[6]

Tim's blog comment the following day was a helpful self-reflection that his primary gifts are indeed oral and rhetorical rather than written: "And even the statement that my book disappointed her in comparison to my preaching is actually true—I'm a better speaker than writer, and always will be. That was more a compliment to the preaching than a criticism of the book."[7]

Tim believes passionately that the conversion of the individual and the transformation of the city come through the preaching of the gospel.

WHAT MAKES TIM KELLER A GOOD COMMUNICATOR?

Tim's verbal gifts have been summarized as follows by Josh Harris:

> To be a great preacher, one needs to be tri-perspectival in . . . exegesis. That is, [one needs] to be committed to the exegesis of the Bible, the exegesis of our culture, and the exegesis of the human heart. Some preachers claim that if you exegete the Bible properly, you don't need to bother yourself with the exegesis of our culture or the human heart. The problem with this view, however, is that the Bible itself exhorts us to apply Biblical norms to both our lives and to our world. . . . But no preacher has consistently taught me how to do all three in the context of every sermon more so than Tim Keller. His balanced attention to all three forms of exegesis makes him very unique, in my opinion.[8]

The following comments mainly concern a sermon titled "Who Is This Jesus?" based on John 9.[9]

Maintain a sustained and substantiated argument. Tim brings together two key statements in a single thesis: "Jesus Christ is both intellectually credible and existentially satisfying." The sermon proceeds to marshal the evidence to engage the hearer's mind and spirit.

The emphasis of the Christian apologetic is that it is relevant because it is true, not because "it works for me." The sermon is not argumentative; instead, it leaves the hearer little option other than to agree with the logic of the Christian's position. As the apostle Paul has argued,

> The weapons we fight with are not the weapons of the world. On the contrary, they have divine power to demolish strongholds. We demolish arguments and every pretension that sets itself up against the knowledge of God, and we take captive every thought to make it obedient to Christ. (2 Corinthians 10:4-5)

Such careful demolition also takes place in Tim's preaching!

Read the culture and its books. Tim's first point was taken from a study of the world's great religions.[10] There are only two tremendous lives: Buddha and Jesus Christ.

Both these men have had divinity ascribed to them. However, the difference between the two was that not only did Jesus Christ claim divinity but others ascribed divinity to him. By contrast, Buddha pointed away from himself, saying that he was not divine, even though others thought him so. In Jesus Christ there is a match-up between his own incredible claims about himself and the claims of his followers.

In another talk, titled "Doing Justice," Tim urges his audience to become well read. When you listen to and read only one thinker, you become a clone. If you listen to and read two thinkers, you will begin to develop your own voice. But when you hear two or three hundred thinkers, you become wise and develop your own voice.[11]

Use memorable and challenging illustrations. Tim used two particularly memorable illustrations to provoke his listeners to act on what they had heard. First he said, "There is such a thing as a placebo effect." We know that it is possible for the mind to be persuaded through suggestion of something that is not true. But the effect is only temporary and does not result in real change. How do you know that what you think is true is not just a placebo? You need to check it out.[12]

Second, he invites his audience to imagine two scenarios. You receive notification that the IRS owes you $100,000 dollars, or you receive a letter stating that you are a long-lost relative of the monarchy. Both claims seem incredible. But because the stakes are so high, you want to find out. The same is true of the tremendous claims of Jesus Christ. Because the stakes are so high, you will want to find out the truth.

Tim does not pepper his sermon with lots of illustrations, but these two, well-placed and memorable as they are, clearly substantiate his point.

Preach in order to persuade. Tim acknowledges that the Christian faith makes demands of people, and that it may seem to be incredible, but he argues, "It is hard to believe who [Christ] is, but it is harder not to do so."

"You haven't met the real Jesus if your reactions are not extreme," he says. You will hate him, love him or fear him. He parodies C. S. Lewis's famous "Mad, bad or God" argument.[13]

Tim regularly returns to his central theme, that Jesus Christ is "existentially satisfying; intellectually credible."

Dr. Stephen Um, a Boston pastor, is quoted in a *New York Times* article commenting on Tim Keller: "You need to enter into a person's worldview, challenge that worldview and retell the story based on the gospel. The problem is evangelicals have always started with challenging the worldview. We don't have any credibility."[14]

Tim anticipates objections and responds to them in his rhetoric. Throughout his sermon he says things such as: "Some of you think"; "Some of you are surprised"; "Some of you are saying, 'my stereotypes have been shattered.' "

He says such things to challenge neutrality and complacency. He won't allow the audience to be indifferent, and forces them to ask the question: What if this was true? Sermons need to persuade. But the aim isn't mere intellectual assent, rather persuasion leading to genuine life change.

The distinctive thing about a sermon is that it is biblical teaching which is not only explained but also calls for decision and action, and is applied to the hearer. For these reasons, the forty-minute talk "Who Is This Jesus?" is better described as a sermon than a lecture. Tim is erudite and well read, dismantling philosophical objections to Christianity. However, he does not leave his argument there but provokes the hearer to make a personal, faith-based response. This is what turns a theological lecture into a biblical sermon.

LESSONS FOR PREACHERS

- Anticipate objections. Preaching is not a dialogue, but neither is it a monologue. In that best-known of all Jesus' sermons he used the little refrain: "You have heard that it was said. . . . But I tell you" (Matthew 5:21-22).

- Read thoroughly and widely. Use your reading to develop your own voice, not to become a clone. Also use your reading to understand the Bible, the culture and the human heart, and demonstrate that your observations are not merely subjective.

- Create intrigue. The goal of the sermon is faith, but that is often achieved by attracting people to the logic and persuasiveness of what is preached. Such preaching should make people curious, encouraging them to pursue things further and feel provoked to connect the dots for themselves.

- Preach for a verdict. Tim has tried to convey to other pastors that the hard sell rarely works in the city. Becoming a Christian in a place like New York is more often the product not just of one decision but of many little decisions. Because we preach the gospel to both Christian and non-Christian, we may bring home gospel-based implications every time we preach.

3

JOHN PIPER

Inspire a Passion for the Glory of God

John Piper is the pastor for preaching at Bethlehem Baptist Church in Minneapolis, Minnesota. He is married to Noël and they have four sons, one daughter and a growing number of grandchildren. Bethlehem is a church which has grown significantly in recent decades: around five thousand people attend each week, representing growth of 1,000 percent in the thirty years that Piper has been pastor. Despite these impressive statistics, Bethlehem does not fit the mold of many American megachurches.

In February 2000 I had a chance to visit BBC for their annual pastors' conference.[1] What impressed me were the church's humble building, challenging urban location and servant-hearted staff team. This is a church which is singularly identified by the regular and faithful pulpit ministry of John Piper. He is author of more than fifty books and is a popular conference and convention speaker. But, supremely, he is the regular week-in-week-out pastor/teacher of his congregation.

John's life mission statement, adopted by BBC, is "God is

most glorified in us when we are most satisfied in Him." With echoes of his hero, Jonathan Edwards, John's plea is for a pervasive God-centeredness in all of life and worship. He contends that our satisfaction, pleasure and delight are not ultimately at odds with God's design for us. God not only wants us to be holy, but also to be happy.

However, in March 2010 John Piper announced to his congregation that he would be taking a time of extended absence from public ministry, not for writing but rather for a "reality check from the Holy Spirit." His specific hope was that the last five years or more of his public ministry prior to retirement might be the most fruitful. He wrote:

> Personally, I view these months as a kind of re-launch of what I hope will be the most humble, happy, and fruitful five years of our 35 years at Bethlehem and 46 years of marriage. . . . May God make these eight months the best Bethlehem has ever known. It would be just like God to do the greatest things when I am not there. "Neither he who plants nor he who waters is anything, but only God who gives the growth" (1 Corinthians 3:7).

WHAT MAKES JOHN PIPER A GOOD COMMUNICATOR?

There is considerable overlap between John's writings and his preaching. Clearly, more of the passion and energy can be communicated in preaching, but, as we shall see, there are a few big themes which occur both in written and spoken form.

Seek your own joy. Bethlehem Baptist Church amplifies John's personal goals in its mission statement: "To spread a passion for the supremacy of God in all things for the joy of all peoples through Jesus Christ."[2]

John states: "[Christian hedonism] comes as close as anything to summing up my entire theology."[3] The idea of Christian hedonism is found in his book *Desiring God*, and has been the main theme of much of his preaching throughout his ministry.

John takes the answer to question one of the Westminster Shorter Catechism and reinterprets it as follows: "The chief end of man is to glorify God *by* [replacing the original word *and*] enjoying Him forever."[4] His argument is that happiness is not an added extra in the Christian life but a core necessity: "I came to see that it is unbiblical and arrogant to try to worship God for any other reason than the pleasure to be had in him."[5]

This theology, he believes, has antecedents in the writings of C. S. Lewis, Jonathan Edwards and Blaise Pascal. Pascal writes, for example:

> All men [and women] seek happiness. This is without exception. Whatever different means they employ, they all tend to this end. The cause of some going to war, and of others avoiding it, is the same desire in both, attended with different views. The will never takes the least step but to this object. This is the motive of every action of every man, even of those who hang themselves.[6]

In *The Pleasures of God*, John points out that God does everything to bring himself pleasure. Indeed, "God's chief end is to glorify God and enjoy himself forever." God takes delight in his Son; he has so made creation to bring him pleasure and glory; he sovereignly elects in order that peoples from every nation will come to bring him glory. Indeed, God does all things for his own pleasure!

Doing something to gain pleasure yourself, far from insulting the receiver of the gift, actually dignifies them. This is illustrated in two ways, in a comment by C. S. Lewis and an illustration of John's own.

In *Reflections on the Psalms*, C. S. Lewis wrote:

> I had never noticed that all enjoyment spontaneously overflows into praise. . . . The world rings with praise—lovers praising their mistresses, readers praising their favourite poet, walkers praising the countryside, players praising their favourite game. . . . I think we delight to praise what we enjoy because the praise not merely expresses but completes the enjoyment; it is its appointed consummation.[7]

According to Lewis, praise is not merely an activity that issues because the object of praise is worthy, but also because the act of praise itself completes the joy and delight!

John uses the following illustration many times in his sermons. It is recorded in the later edition of *Desiring God* (which I have taken the liberty of paraphrasing slightly):

> Suppose I come home to my wife on our wedding anniversary with a big bunch of red roses. When she opens the door, flinging her arms around me and thanking me for the gift, I could make one of two responses. If I say to her, "I had to buy these for you—it is my duty; at wedding anniversaries these are the things husbands are supposed to do," she would probably not be very impressed! If, however, I respond by saying, "Darling I love you, and it gives me great pleasure to give you flowers," she will not turn to me and say, "How selfish you are talking about *your* pleas-

ure." But rather she will respond positively, seeing that the pleasure I gain from giving her flowers dignifies both the act and the action!⁸

This illustration demonstrates the dignity that self-seeking delight in God gives to the concept of Christian hedonism. Now, this is a particular challenge to a stoical British preacher like me! Do I see joy as central to authentic worship of God, not as a foolhardy distraction, at worst, or an added extra, at best? And do I preach in such a way that the congregation seeks joy in God?

Use arresting and shocking language. John uses phrases and terminology which provoke a reaction. To ascribe the word *hedonism* to authentic Christian worship elicits a retort from many hearers. He takes this word which has negative connotations for most people and turns its meaning on its head. Hedonism means "pleasure seeking," and as an end in itself, it is the epitome of human-centered self-seeking. For example, the word translated "pleasure" or "lusts" in James 4:3, "When you ask, you do not receive, because you ask with wrong motives, that you may spend what you get on your pleasures," comes from the root *hēdonē*, from which we get the English word "hedonism."

Many have objected that redefining hedonism in this way causes a distraction and may lead to confusion. It is a word that makes me feel uncomfortable. But it also makes me think. It challenges me to consider the key concept which underpins John's reading of the Bible: God's desire for his own glory and the Christian's active pursuit of happiness in God. This is preaching that shocks and jars, causing the congregation to sit up and listen, to question and consider.

Other memorable phrases John uses include: "God is most glorified in us when we are most satisfied in Him"; "Life is war"; and "Mission exists because worship doesn't." Preachers need to lodge biblical thoughts in their congregations' minds through such memorable comments.

Be God-centered. This point is forcefully made in John Piper's *The Supremacy of God in Preaching*: "Preaching that does not have the aroma of God's greatness may entertain for a season, but it will not touch the hidden cry of the soul: 'Show me thy glory!'"[9]

This model of preaching is reminiscent of the style of the New England pastor Jonathan Edwards. *The Supremacy of God in Preaching* contains the following themes: stirring up holy affections, enlightening the mind, saturating with Scripture, employing analogies, using threats and warnings, pleading for a response, probing the workings of the heart, yielding to the Holy Spirit in prayer, being broken and tender-hearted, and being intense.[10]

These central themes regularly remind the reader that the cure for the soul's ills is preaching, which reveal to the hearer the majesty of God. Only as God is set forth in all his glory will our hunger for him be satisfied. "God will hide from you much of the fruit he causes in your ministry," says John. "You'll see enough to be assured of his blessing, but not so much as to think you could live without it. For God aims to exalt himself, not the preacher."[11]

Find historical associations. John Piper followed the advice of his seminary professor and chose to make one great theologian his lifetime's study. That great theologian was Jonathan Edwards. John comments:

Does any of us know what an incredible thing it is that this man, who was a small-town pastor for 23 years in a church of 600 people, a missionary to Indians for 7 years, who reared 11 faithful children, who worked without the help of electric light, or word-processors or quick correspondence, or even sufficient paper to write on, who lived only until he was 54, and who died with a library of 300 books—that this man led one of the greatest awakenings of modern times, wrote theological books that have ministered for 200 years and did more for the modern missionary movement than anyone of his generation?[12]

In Jonathan Edwards we find a combination of mind-stretching doctrine with heartwarming preaching:

A truly practical or saving faith, is light and heat together, or rather light and love, while that which is only a speculative faith, is only light without heat; and, in that it wants spiritual heat or divine love, is in vain, and good for nothing. A speculative faith consists only in the assent of the understanding; but in a saving faith which is only of the former kind, is no better than the faith of devils for they have faith so far as it can exist without love, believing while they tremble.[13]

John's life mission statement about God being most glorified in us when we are most satisfied with him is taken from the theology of Jonathan Edwards, as this quote would seem to demonstrate:

God is glorified not only by His glory being seen, but by its being rejoiced in. When those that see it delight in it, God is more glorified than if they only see it. His glory is then received by the whole soul, both by the understanding and by the heart. God made the world that He might communicate, and the creature receive, His glory; and that it might [be] received both by the mind and heart. He that testifies also his idea of God's glory [doesn't] glorify God so much as that testifies also his approbation of it and his delight in it.[14]

The central relationship between love for God, love for self and love for others intertwines the preaching of both Edwards and John.[15] To say to a modern audience, It is your Christian duty to find your joy in God, sounds very contemporary, but in fact this may be found in great preaching from the past. Knowing that adds weight and substance to this point.

Continue to refine central themes to make them clearer. In a sermon given at Mars Hill Church in Seattle on February 26, 2010, John summarized what, as we've already seen, he felt was his single life theme: "God's glory, the honor of his name and his supremacy in all things and how this relates to my personal satisfaction in God."[16] His central question was, Does God's love for me mean that God makes much of me?

He traced the big themes of the Bible, focused around the major acts of God's love: predestination (Ephesians 1:5); creation (Isaiah 43:6-7); incarnation (Luke 2:10-11; 2 Corinthians 5:21); sanctification (Philippians 1:9-11); propagation (Romans 1:5); consummation (2 Thessalonians 1:9). These biblical themes, for John, pose the key question: Do you feel more loved by God because he makes much of you, or because at great cost to himself he frees you to enjoy making much of him forever?

Texts like these indicate that God does indeed make much of you and me. We need to hear the force of the biblical text that God loves us to such a great extent that he sent his Son for us.

He sent his Son to seek and to save the lost, the Son who washed the disciples' feet, and he rejoices over us.

But the big challenge, arising from the Bible and explored in John's sermon, is: Am I only making much of God *because* he is making much of me? John makes the key point that all glory in life is to be deflected back to him: "He makes much of me for his glory"; "No one goes to the Grand Canyon to increase his self-esteem"; "Your feeling of being valued will not be your God; it will provide the security of helping you behold God's glory."

It seems to me that this sermon summarizes one of John's key themes in his rewording of the first question of the Westminster Shorter Catechism.

One very good illustration from this sermon, which John has used on several occasions to reiterate this central point, is the difference between a microscope and a telescope:

> Magnify him, but not like a microscope. You know the difference between two kinds of magnification, don't you? There's telescope magnification and microscope magnification, and it's blasphemy to magnify God like a microscope. To magnify God like a microscope is to take something tiny and make it look bigger than it is. If you try to do that to God, you blaspheme. But a telescope puts its lens on unimaginable expanses of greatness and tries to just help them look like what they are. That's what a telescope is for.[17]

The central theme of John's life's preaching is reapplied to a specific time and used to answer concerns and objections.

LESSONS FOR PREACHERS

- Apply Bible truth through the head to the heart. Our preaching should be marked by "heat" (passion) and "light" (illumination). It is not enough to "teach the Bible." The preacher's task is not complete until the message has affected will and emotions as well as intellect.

- If it is true, then be passionate about it! God-centered preaching should not leave the preacher unmoved. The congregation will connect well if they know that you have met with God in your preparation, and, more significantly, they too will meet with God as you preach.

- Repreach the same passages or biblical themes until they are clear in your own mind. I have listened to Dick Lucas preach over several decades and am surprised at how much he preaches and repreaches the same passage and the same thing, yet there is always freshness and new insight. But essentially the big theme (particularly from the Gospel of Mark, in his case) is repeated. All too often I leave the pulpit thinking, "I wish I could do that over again; it is only now becoming clear to me as I sit down." John and others would encourage us to keep reworking big Bible themes until they are crystal clear and seen with fresh application for today.

Sources
For MP3 audio of John Piper sermons: www.desiringgod.org

Key books by John Piper:
Desiring God. Colorado Springs: Multnomah Books, 1996.
The Pleasures of God. Colorado Springs: Multnomah Press, 1991.
The Purifying Power of Living by Faith in Future Grace. Colorado Springs: Multnomah Press, 1995.
God's Passion for His Glory. Wheaton, Ill.: Crossway Books, 1998.
The Dangerous Duty of Delight. Colorado Springs: Multnomah Publishers, 2001.
The Supremacy of God in Preaching. Grand Rapids: Baker, 2004.

4

VAUGHAN ROBERTS

Let the Bible Speak with
Simplicity and Freshness

Vaughan Roberts is the rector of St. Ebbe's Church, Oxford, England, where he initially served as a curate under Rev. David Fletcher, after graduating with a degree in law and theology from Cambridge University. It is exceptional for a curate to take over from the rector. Another noted exception was the late John Stott, who moved from the position as curate of All Souls Langham Place, London, to being its rector.[1] John Stott is an incomparable model of a biblical expositor. One aspect of his preaching, however, seems to have found lineage in Vaughan Roberts, namely, the comprehensive treatment of a biblical text, following which the listener is left with a sense that the depth of the text has been mined and clearly presented. It is perhaps for this reason that Vaughan credits John Stott as being a major influence in his preaching.

Vaughan is the director of Proclamation Trust, an organization founded by Dick Lucas in order to encourage expository preaching. Through this preaching method, the argument goes, it is God who sets the agenda. Proclamation Trust encourages expository preaching through its conferences and the annual Evangelical Ministry Assembly in London. Vaughan is also the author of nine books at the time of this writing.[2] Preaching, however, is his major ministry and takes up the best part of his working week. He explains,

> I never really wanted to do anything but be a pastor-teacher after I was converted in my later teens but, being very shy at the time, I couldn't imagine that anyone else would think I could do it. Helping at camps for teenagers gave me opportunities to give short Bible talks. That led to more invitations and encouragement from people I respected that I did have some embryonic preaching gifts.[3]

Vaughan's own thoughts on preaching have been recorded for the Evangelical Alliance website.[4] He practices a systematic and consecutive exposition of a Bible book. In order to prepare for a new sermon series, he advocates reading the Bible book over and over again, asking oneself the question, *What is the thrust and what are some of the main themes?* "You cannot get the message today before you have got the message then. In this way you will find it has many applications," he says. Vaughan tries to follow Charles Simeon's goal: "My endeavour is to bring out of Scripture what is there and not to thrust in what I think might be there. I have a great jealousy on this head: never to speak more or less than I believe to be the mind of the Spirit in the passage I'm expounding."[5]

Vaughan has many opportunities to preach around the United Kingdom. But he preaches a sermon series first at St. Ebbe's week by week before preaching it anywhere else. This is important, he believes, not least because it is through preaching that Christ rules his church and builds up the local church community. Because the Bible first addresses communities, not individuals, so the preaching of the Bible should happen in the local church community initially.

Vaughan Roberts's linkage of the Word and the world is again shaped by John Stott, who wrote, "The preacher is a bridge-builder relating God's never-changing word to our ever-changing world."[6] Vaughan argues that unless the preacher is absolutely convinced that preaching matters, he will not find the time to prepare properly for it. And it is a massive effort week by week to carve out time for preparation.

The vision for training preachers (through the Proclamation Trust and the 9:38 Apprentice Scheme) is a natural outworking of Vaughan's own conviction about the centrality of preaching in the life of the gathered congregation.[7]

WHAT MAKES VAUGHAN ROBERTS A GOOD COMMUNICATOR?

What follows is a study on Vaughan's sermon on Romans 11:36: "For from him and through him and to him are all things. To him be the glory forever! Amen." It is a great model of a clearly structured sermon outline that serves the biblical text.[8]

Help the congregation see where you are heading. Vaughan begins by announcing and reading his text. "Textual" preaching was once the favored evangelical way: a single Bible text used as the basis of all that followed. While it is good to have varieties of approaches to preaching the Bible, using a single verse is a very effective way to ensure that the congregation leave with a portion of Scripture firmly lodged in their minds. Vaughan makes it clear that the ensuing sermon will be focused around the single theme derived from this text.

Use a good introduction. Vaughan begins the sermon with a joke. Passengers are told that they are the first people to fly on a fully automated, pilotless plane. But they need not worry because "nothing can go wrong . . . nothing can go wrong . . . nothing can go wrong."

It was not the funniest joke in the world, but it works well because it leads effectively into the point that despite our mistaken confidence in our own ability, we really cannot control our plans. "You will have discovered that what is true for us is true of great world leaders too," says Vaughan. But, though we cannot control our future, God controls the beginning and the end. It is important that the opening joke or story is tied to the big questions people are asking.

Vaughan continues, "Is what is true for us individually and naturally also true of the world generally? Are we on a pilotless plane? The atheist is bound to say that there is no flight plan. But there is a God ultimately in control, and nothing can go wrong. God is in control."

Next, Vaughan turns to the context of Romans 11, for in this chapter there are big questions which need to be addressed. Here there is even a big question mark over whether God is in control at all.[9]

The Old Testament seems to talk about the great plan of God, a God who made promises to Abraham, which began with Israel and were ultimately fulfilled with the coming of Christ the Messiah.

Paul preached first to the Jews, but the majority of them rejected the message. Hence the big question: Is God really in control? Paul writes these chapters to affirm that God can indeed be trusted. Nothing in the end can go wrong. Paul will conclude by encouraging us to join in the adoring worship of our God.

Make three points using mnemonic, alliteration and repetition. Vaughan invites the congregation to consider three main points. We note that he spends most of his time addressing the complicated exegetical points of the passage, expecting the congregation to follow his thinking with an open Bible in front of them.

1. The conclusion of God's plan—that all Israel will be saved (Romans 11:25-27). This passage contains a horticultural metaphor. A cultured olive tree (Israel) and a wild olive tree (Gentiles) are grafted together. God is not starting again: he has taken branches out of the wild tree and grafted them in and lopped off others.

Gentiles must not be proud and assume that God has finished with the Jews. Vaughan is addressing his largely Gentile congregation: "No, you are weeds; you're wild and God has graciously planted you in. He hasn't finished with Israel. Israel's rejection is partial and temporary. In the amazing providence of God, Israel's rejection leads to Gentile inclusion. Paul expects that many Jews will look on and long for inclusion."

A tricky verse to interpret is: "All Israel will be saved" (v. 26). What does Paul mean by Israel? Elsewhere Paul talks about the church becoming the true people of God, the children of Abraham (Romans 4). In Galatians 6 the church is described as the Israel of God. Is that what Paul means here?

Vaughan continues by stating that we need to notice that whenever Paul talks of Israel in Romans 9–11 (e.g., 11:25), he means Jews. But "all Israel will be saved need not mean every single individual. Rather the nation as a whole. The remnant of believers is composed of those Jews in every generation who will believe (rather than a turning at the end of time)."

At the same time, Paul imagines that this is building to a climax and that one day the great majority will believe. Verse 15 seems to be Paul's great expectation for the end of time.

2. *The goal of God's plan—that all people may receive mercy (Romans 11:28-32).* As he leads the congregation through these sometimes controversial verses, Vaughan acknowledges again that some of the teaching of Romans 9–11 has been hard to understand and hard to accept. He also says at one point, "If I've lost you, come back," encouraging the congregation that even if the detail of the argument is complex, nevertheless there are important truths in there for everyone, and these truths are worthy of their concentration.

A particularly difficult part is the teaching about the sovereignty of God. Vaughan hopes that this teaching will lead the congregation to praise God. The main emphasis is on God's sovereign mercy, and even when God hardens some, he does it in order to extend his mercy to others.

Verse 28 offers two perspectives. From the perspective of the gospel, the Jews are enemies: God is using their rejection in order for the gospel to come to the Gentiles. But from the perspective of election, they are loved on account of the Patriarchs.

God has not abandoned his plans, and he is determined to extend his mercy to all. The disobedience of the Jews will show that they are in exactly the same place as the Gentiles (in need of God's mercy). God has given all men and women over to disobedience so that he may have mercy on them all. But this does not mean that everyone will receive the mercy of God (all without *distinction*, not all without *exception*).[10]

Vaughan uses the illustration of a school awards program, where those who win awards do so on the basis of merit. A lot of people imagine that heaven will be like that, but really it would be terrible if that was so!

However, heaven is not like this: no one actually deserves a place in the presence of God. "God places us in the prison of disobedience that he might have mercy on us all—whoever we are, whatever our race, whatever we have done. This is a wonderful message, for every type of person."

For those of us who are used to success, it means my saying, "I am a failure," "I am a rebel." It is very hard to say this, but that is what is needed. The basis of acceptance is not merit but mercy.

Thus Vaughan concludes his second point: "I am bound to ask you—have you received that gift?"

3. The response to God's plan—that all glory goes to God (Romans 11:33-36). This third point focuses on the appropriate response to the theology contained in these verses. Says Vaughan, "It is deep theology, isn't it? Now pause and reflect and be amazed at the great God I have been speaking of. This passage is not designed to make us debate the minor points. The goal is worship. Note verse 33."

God's judgments are unsearchable, so you will never work them out or think your way to God. We are used to the idea that our reason is the ultimate arbiter. We decide what we will accept or reject. Some do it very arrogantly; others offer Jesus advice like a politician's public relations director. Commenting on verse 34, Vaughan says, "How dare you presume to give advice to God? Sometimes we can almost think we are doing God a favor. We treat him rather like the aging dog; he should be so thankful that we are treating him well when everyone else is ignoring him."

God does not need you (v. 36). He is the source, sustainer and goal of everything. Every breath we take is by divine enabling. The universe is not a stage on which we show off our great talents. It is a stage for the glory of God. Our lives have been given so that people may say what an amazing God he is.

APPLICATION

Vaughan reminds the congregation that these truths should lead us to worship. He challenges the congregation to pray, particularly for Jewish people to come to faith.

He makes two further points of application:

- The goal of God's plan is that all people should receive mercy. "This should make me humble; I am just a worm whom Jesus has saved. For the sins of today I deserve to go to hell," he says.

- Our response to God's plan is to be that all glory will go to him. What are the goals for the rest of our lives? The danger is that we write the script, ensuring that we are the stars of the show. "The rest of our life becomes about gaining applause for ourselves. But that is paganism, not Christianity. The goal of my life is to show off the glory of God."

We've looked at a fairly detailed synopsis of Vaughan's sermon for two reasons. First, Vaughan preaches a content-driven sermon. The text from Romans 11 requires sustained concentration in order to follow the careful logic. Second, Vaughan provides an excellent model of a traditional homiletical form, so it is valuable to see the coherent structure of the sermon. It may be summarized as follows:

Sermon Outline on Romans 11:25-36

Introduction

    Announce the text (v. 36)

    Tell the joke and link into the theme of the sermon

First point

    The conclusion of God's plan: That all Israel will be saved (vv. 2-27)

Second point

    The goal of God's plan: That all people may receive mercy (vv. 28-32)

Third point

    The response to God's plan: That all glory goes to God (vv. 33-36)

Conclusion

    The goal of God's plan: That all people should receive mercy

    Our response to God's plan: That all glory will go to God

This is the skeletal structure spoken of by Charles Simeon, for the most part hidden under the flesh and clothing of the sermon, but essential for holding everything together.[11]

LESSONS FOR PREACHERS

- Carefully interact with the Bible text in such a way that the passage is the controlling agenda for the shape and substance of the sermon. The mark of a good sermon is one that enables the congregation to leave with a clear understanding of the passage in their minds.

- Have a clear, detailed structure for the sermon that supports your argument in the biblical text. But it is probably not ready to be written up, rehearsed and memorized until the sermon outline can be written on a single side of paper.

- Be economical and precise with your use of words. Choose

these carefully and sharpen the point you are making by being clear in your own mind about which words work best.

- Mentor a new generation of preachers. As Vaughan has done at St. Ebbe's Church and through the Proclamation Trust, give young preachers an opportunity to preach, providing training beforehand and feedback afterward.

5

SIMON PONSONBY

Be a Word-and-Spirit Preacher

Simon Ponsonby left the meat industry to become an evangelist, before training for ordination in the Church of England. He has been pastor of theology at St. Aldate's in Oxford, England, since 2005, a role that combines teaching, traveling and writing. He is married to Tiffany, and they have two sons. His sermons have been known to include various bits of butchered meat, including a massive ox tongue to demonstrate that the human tongue, though smaller, has more power to do good and to destroy. This also serves as a good metaphor in a chapter on the need to be a Word-and-Spirit preacher.

Simon is the author of three books. Both these and his preaching are marked by a desire to be well-reasoned theologically, coupled with a challenge to continue to grow in the love and worship of God. In his second book, *God Inside Out*, Simon wrestles with the challenge of going deeper in the Spirit, which also means going deeper into God's Word, in a way that stimulates both the head and the heart.[1] His books are good models of the evangelical desire that theology should lead to doxology.[2]

There is an unhealthy caricature which can seem to imply that (to put it crudely) expository preaching does not happen in charismatic churches (like St. Aldate's) and that the Holy Spirit is not at work in conservative churches (such as St. Ebbe's, Oxford). It is good to be able to include both Vaughan and Simon in this selection. We've noted Vaughan's application of the doctrine of Romans 11 to the heartfelt response expected from the believer. In what follows, we shall look at the way in which Simon expounds a single biblical text on a doctrinal theme.

WHAT MAKES SIMON PONSONBY A GOOD COMMUNICATOR?

We will consider a sermon Simon preached on the topic of holiness titled "Consecrating Ourselves to the Lord," based on the text where Joshua told the people, "Consecrate yourselves, for tomorrow the LORD will do amazing things among you" (Joshua 3:5).

Tell the congregation what is on your mind. I use the expression "tell them what is on your mind" with caution, lest I be misunderstood. The sermon is not the place for all the "bees in your bonnet" to come out and sting the congregation! As somebody has wisely said, the only difference between a horse and a hobbyhorse is that you can get off a horse!

However, one feature of Simon's preaching is that it is very personal. Simon helps the congregation to see how he has wrestled with the subject. They get the sense that this is truth which has deeply affected his own life, and it is a strength of his preaching that he reveals this impact to the congregation.

Note the repeated use of *I* in the following extracts from Simon's sermon:

I believe that if a people consecrate themselves to God . . . I believe if they will respond to God's five-time invitation to be holy, then he will do amazing things not just in our lives and our family, but in our community and in our society.

I have long been a student of church revival. . . . I became a Christian twenty-five years ago in the context of a localized revival. . . . For less than a year it seemed as though God came down on that church. . . . If one gets saved in that context, one thinks that is normal.

That was not the norm, but I have longed to see it happen not just in one church, but in the nation too. . . . I have spent many years reading on revival but have never seen it.

But I do believe that it is a promise that, if we consecrate ourselves to him tomorrow, God will do extraordinary things. . . . God is consistent with his Word and his ways. . . . People are hungry for [revival].

This is a message Simon has clearly first preached to himself and sought to apply personally.

Establish the parameters for your talk. Simon preaches on a big theme. It is important to him to define at the beginning of this sermon exactly what he intends to cover.

Consecration is "setting apart things as holy. . . . The church is good at most things apart from holiness."

Simon confesses: "I have been a Christian for twenty-five years. I have learnt a lot of things . . . but I was reflecting: How much more like the Lord am I now than I was twenty years ago?"

Consecration is the demarcating of a people or a place or a time exclusively to God. It is devotion to God, set apart for God. It is a withdrawing, not from society. It is a movement away from sin, not away from sinners.

Simon makes it clear to the congregation that he does not intend to exhaust the teaching on holiness, but rather bring home the personal implications for them.

Build a theological case for a big-themed sermon. The big problem that the sermon seeks to address is the lack of holiness and consecration in the church: "We can be so busy about church stuff that we lose God."

The primary attribute of God is holiness (not love). The angels were not crying, "Love is all you need"; they were crying, "Holy, holy, holy."

The rest of the sermon is not so much an exegesis of Joshua 3:5 as a theological examination of the big theme of consecration/holiness. This structure is analogous to eating an apple. Notice the way that Simon works around the key theme until he gets to the core.

1. Consecration brings visitation. Three examples from the Bible make this point.

First, Simon says, Moses encouraged consecration in preparation for God's coming. Following their consecration, the Holy Spirit then fell on seventy of their leaders, and they all began prophesying (a reference to Numbers 11).

Second, he makes the point that "Joshua built and God came." As they were coming to the edge of the Promised Land, the people were encouraged by Joshua to devote themselves to God. The waters parted, and the people marched into the land.

Third, Jesus said in Acts 1: "Wait for the gift my Father promised." The people devoted themselves to prayer, waited on God and consecrated themselves. Then on Pentecost Day, God's

Spirit fell, just as he had when he fell on Moses. This was the greater fulfillment of the promise made to the seventy in Numbers 11.

2. *Consecration must begin at the house of God.* Simon urges the congregation to realize that consecration must start with us. God's promises are not addressed to the sinner or to the secular world. The call is to God's people.

Simon quotes 2 Chronicles 7:14 several times, with an emphasis on the word *if.* If his people will do four things—humble themselves, pray, seek his face (not his hand; it is intimate, personal encounter) and turn from their sins—then God will hear them from heaven, forgive their sins and heal their land.

Quoting John Henry Newman, he says: "The church often starts out as a prophet and ends up as a policeman." We're called to be salt and light, but often we are the judge and jury. God doesn't expect the world to be holy. But he does expect saints to be holy.

God starts with his people. Jesus began his public ministry by cleansing the temple and casting out demons. Revival happens first in God's church before it reforms the wider world. "Sadly holiness is often all too far from the church's agenda," says Simon.

3. *We have tried everything but consecration.* Simon points out that the idea of holiness is a vast biblical theme, and that the word and its cognates occur 850 times in the Old Testament and 150 times in the New, but he claims, "[ironically] we never discussed holiness in theological college."

> We've tried everything. Between 1997 and 2005 half a million members stopped going to church altogether. . . . Spin results in hemorrhaging in the church . . . We need

God to become the attraction in church. . . . Don't you think we should give holiness a go?

At every point in the sermon Simon applies the argument to the congregation. The hearers feel his emphasis that this is not for information only. He is earnest and expecting that his preaching will result in change, and he urges for the latter as he speaks.

4. *A holy church can create a holy society.* This fourth point is not made from a particular text but rather by applying the previous three points.

Simon argues that if Christians are to be the salt of the earth, rubbed into the fabric of society, then we can make a real difference. He quotes Jim Wallis: "The social transformation of the world . . . can only come through a spiritual revival."

Simon believes that a transformed church transforms society, and that where God is at work society will change. The moral state of society is indicative of the moral state of the church.

Illustrate from history and contemporary media. There were a number of illustrations throughout the sermon. Simon commented on the Kevin Costner film *Field of Dreams*, and from it repeated on several occasions the phrase "If you build it, he will come." The phrase is central to the plot, where Iowa farmer Ray Kinsella hears a voice say the words, and interprets this as a message telling him to build a baseball field on his cornfield.

Delving into history, Simon quoted Welsh revivalist Evan Roberts, from "Consecrate Yourselves to the Lord," stressing that there are a number of things that need to happen before revival comes: confess before God every sin in your past life; remove everything that is doubtful in your life; totally surrender (say and do everything the Spirit leads you to say and do); and publicly profess Christ.[3]

Simon also illustrates from John Wesley in Oxford in 1734. The point is that in order to change in the world the congregation needs to know that revival starts with individual change, followed by the transformation of the church, and subsequently the reformation of culture. Wesley said, "My one aim in life is to secure personal holiness, for without being holy myself I cannot promote real holiness in others." Simon expands this to apply it directly to students at the University of Oxford: "The devil hates it when people get serious with God. He hates holiness. Indeed when revival did break out in Oxford under Wesley, some undergraduates were kicked out of the university. Imagine being sent down for being too holy!"

Simon also argues that English revivals led to the reform of society in the 1850s. The Welsh Revival had a similar effect, and so too did revivals associated with Billy Sunday and Billy Graham.

Ask the practical question: How do we do it? As he draws the sermon to a close, Simon presents some challenges:

"Does everyone you work with know you are a Christian?"

"Someone has to say, 'I am going for holiness.' "

"Can you say, 'I will be that person'? If we consecrate ourselves, God will do amazing, marvellous things."

A. W. Tozer said, "You are as holy as you want to be."

Henry Vardy said to D. L. Moody, "The world has yet to see what God can do through a man fully devoted to him."

LESSONS FOR PREACHERS

- Preach big theological themes from the Bible. This will involve more than the careful exegesis of one Bible passage. Such sermons are not easy to preach, but they are important, helping the congregation to construct a theological theme from the Bible in a coherent way.

- Preach in such a way that you can pray for and expect the Spirit to be at work. Pray, too, over the Word you preach. Dr. Martyn Lloyd-Jones describes the experience of the sacred anointing:

  > The one thing needed above all else is the accompanying power of the Spirit. . . . It is "power from on high." It is the preacher gliding on eagles' wings, soaring high, swooping low, carrying and being carried along by a dynamic other than his own. His consciousness of what is happening is not obliterated. He is not in a trance. He is being worked on but is aware that he is still working. He is being spoken through but he knows he is still speaking.[4]

- Expect that God will transform the congregation through the very message you have preached. If we preachers expect God the Holy Spirit to be at work through the preaching of the Word, then we should allow space and time after the sermon so that the Word penetrates the heart, and pray that Satan will not snatch away what has been carefully sown (Mark 4:15).

6

Use Humor and Story to Connect and Engage, and Dismantle Barriers

J.John is a Greek Cypriot living in Chorleywood, Hertfordshire, England. His preaching ministry as an itinerant evangelist has wide appeal, not least because of the down-to-earth and humorous way in which his messages are presented. He is married to Killy, and they have three sons.

J.John's talks are peppered with humor, stories and anecdotes, but it would not be fair to conclude from this that his preaching is therefore entertainment without substance. The messages are not light, and the content speaks much about sin. J.John says, "What I want to do is to make people laugh, so that they will take things seriously." He appeals for personal conversion and radically altered lives.

The "Just 10" preaching series attracted huge crowds, and an estimated one million people have attended so far. Given that the theme is the Ten Commandments, such huge popularity has come as something of a surprise. There are two striking ways in which the message has been presented. First, J.John counts down from the tenth to the first over ten evenings of talks. The second is that the commandment is rephrased with a positive message: 10. Find Contentment; 9. Hold to the Truth; 8. Prosper with a Clear Conscience; 7. Affair-Proof Your Relationships; 6. Manage Your Anger; 5. Keep the Peace with Your Parents; 4. Catch Your Breath; 3. Take God Seriously; 2. Know God; 1. Live by Priorities.

Even the national media have highlighted the dramatic impact of J.John's preaching, recording crowds of people making restitution for wrong, returning stolen property, and dumping pornography and weapons in the massive bins provided. One person even sent £103,000 ($170,000) in cash, accompanied with a note explaining that it was unpaid tax.

Like the other preachers in this book, J.John is unique. It would obviously be foolish to try to adopt his style or personal approach to preaching. Much of his distinctive personality comes through, and his preaching fits the adage "The communication of truth by personality."[1] However, many of the things he does well can actually be learned, adapted and applied.

WHAT MAKES J.JOHN A GOOD COMMUNICATOR?

Tell memorable one-liners. The national press have commented on J.John's "comic timing" and depicted him as a "Christian stand-up comedian." I am not sure whether this description is accurate, but it does recognize J.John's clever use of humor in preaching, much of it through self-deprecation: "[When I became a Christian] my mother said I had been brainwashed. I replied, 'Mum, my brain *has* been washed, and if you knew what had been in my brain you'd be pleased it got washed.'"

J.John summarizes the Christian message in memorable phrases:

The Ten Commandments—God's top 10—are not obsolete, they are absolute.
If you take "Christ" out of "Christian" you are left with "Ian." And Ian isn't going to help you!
The three pillars of the church are worship (look up), well-being (look in) and witness (look out).[2]

Using humor is a risk in sermons. Some people are poor at telling jokes; others are so good at it that they distract from God's message. But we would all agree that humorless sermons are likely to lose an audience's interest very quickly. Few people are able to tell stories and jokes as effectively as J.John, and preachers should be aware of their own limitations and do only what they are able to do well. Nevertheless, humor disarms the audience, enabling people to see their humanity and foibles in a fresh light and allowing the preacher to connect with real life.

We are going to focus on a sermon by J.John titled "Changing in a Changing World," an evangelistic talk based on John 3:1-16.[3]

J.John begins by devoting considerable time to making social and human observations before arriving at the biblical text. He seeks to ensure that he has shown an understanding of the contemporary world, its needs and its faults, before applying the Bible's remedy.

Seek resonance with your audience through human story. "We live in a changing world. Would you agree with that?" asks J.John. (Audible yeses can be heard from the congregation.) To demonstrate this point he lists several changes that have happened in the past seventy years: If you were born before 1940, "a big Mac was an oversized raincoat"; "crumpet was what you had for tea"; "a stud was something you fastened to your wrist"; " 'going all the way' meant staying on the bus all the way to the bus depot"; and "a joint was a piece of meat, and grass was mown."

Everyone is affected by change, says J.John. "Change is inevitable except from a vending machine." But now, he argues, even change is changing. (At this point the humor stops for him to make an important point.) "There is more tolerance for everything, but there is less tolerance of anything that doesn't seem to be tolerant."

Do more than tell a good story; draw out the specific analogy. J.John frequently begins his sermons with a story, to create curiosity and intrigue, and to attract the audience's attention. The following is an example.

Ivan McGuire lived in the exciting and dangerous world of professional skydiving. His job was not only to hurl his body from a plane toward the earth at over one hundred miles per hour, but also to instruct others on how to do the same. Mr. McGuire was a skydiving instructor. In fact, he was so skilled at his profession that he became an instructor of the instructors. Mr. McGuire filmed other teachers and students in freefall and then used the footage to evaluate performances.

By 1988 he had over eight hundred jumps to his credit. That's the same as jumping from an airplane every day for over two years. So it was obviously no big deal when Ivan McGuire jumped out of a plane with camera in hand early in April 1988, ready to film another lesson. But the video he shot that day told a tragic story.

Another instructor and student were seen freefalling for

several seconds before disappearing quickly from view as they pulled their parachute releases, and their chutes deployed. The video showed Mr. McGuire's right hand moving down to pull his own release. But something clearly went wrong. Instead of the expected jerk and sudden deceleration, Mr. McGuire continued to accelerate. The film became blurry and bumpy as he struggled in the air but, in the video, the inevitable was obvious. He was falling toward the earth at nearly 150 miles per hour, and, tragically, he had no way to stop himself.

The final few seconds of the tape were destroyed on impact. Mr. McGuire's body was found in some woods, just over a mile from the airfield. He was not wearing a parachute; he had very tragically forgotten to take it.

J.John proceeds to draw out an analogy and explain how vital it is to take God's instruction for our survival seriously.[4]

Several of the stories in J.John's sermon are familiar. For example, he tells the well-known story of the frog in a pan of hot water. When placed in the water, the frog will immediately jump out. But place a frog in cold water and slowly turn up the heat, and it will die.

However, what makes the story powerful is the way in which a specific analogy is drawn out. "Gradual change is accepted. The changes that can do the most harm are those that we don't see coming. In a way we're all in the same pan. We react immediately to dramatic changes. But we are all at risk if we fail to notice the little changes around us."

It is possible to be a good storyteller but fail to help the congregation see the exact nature of the analogy being made. Good preachers help congregations to connect the dots.

Make good use of repetition and alliteration. J.John uses repetition and alliteration to emphasize the point that certain things have not changed.

1. In a changing world, the nature of God has not changed. Two quotes from the Bible make this point: "I the LORD do not change" (Malachi 3:6) and "Jesus Christ is the same yesterday and today and forever" (Hebrews 13:8).

"God is unchanging in his love. He is unchanging in his judgments. In a world of instability, insecurity and uncertainty it is very good to know that God our Creator is stable; God our Creator is secure."

2. In a changing world, human nature has not changed. Despite our achievements, we are selfish and jealous. We have conquered Everest but not ourselves. J.John quotes from two thinkers to illustrate this point. Albert Einstein wisely observed: "When we released the atom everything changed except our thinking, and so we drift towards unparalleled disaster." J.John says, "Our chief problem has always been ourselves." He backs this up with a quote from Leo Tolstoy: "Everyone thinks of changing humanity; no one thinks of changing themselves."

He leads us to a biblical focus: we are imprisoned by our own strong impulses, a point made in Galatians 5:19-21, where we don't see a pleasant picture of humankind, but an accurate one nonetheless.

J.John makes his comments with verbal bullet points. Through staccato phrases, he repeats and rephrases his second point about unchanging human nature:

> This passage shows us the seriousness of our standing before God. We change jobs, we change partners, but we don't change ourselves. Self-reformation is not enough.

Trying to be good is good, but it is not good enough. What is needed is a radical change in the human heart. The heart of the human problem is the problem of the human heart. We can only change the world by changing people.

3. In a changing world, the way to change hasn't changed. J.John turns to the area of medicine, and specifically Dr. John Rosen and his therapeutic technique for treating psychotic symptoms. Dr. Rosen pioneered a radical approach to treating severely depressed patients. He found that many recovered well when he literally got on to their bed and spent time hugging them. J.John makes the point that, in Christ Jesus, God moves in on the wards. His second quote is from a former director of NASA, Dr. Wernher von Braun: "This creation must have had a maker."

J.John quotes letters that people have written to him, talking about their understanding of the Christian faith. He concludes that it is possible to be religious and not be a Christian. It is possible to know God in a secondhand way.

By combining authorities in medicine and science and personal correspondence, J.John demonstrates that his points are verifiable, both objectively and subjectively.

He concludes by bringing people back to the Bible passage and making the point that it was Jesus Christ who first used the phrase "born again." There is no true believer who has not been born again. Nicodemus was a religious man, but he only knew God in a secondhand way. Many of those who write to J.John are very similar to Nicodemus.

Jesus emphasized three things (again, notice the good use of repetition):

1. The necessity for the new birth. Personal knowledge of God is only possible through being born again (John 3:3, 7). Humans can only reproduce human life, but the Holy Spirit gives new life from heaven, which "means receiving a new life, not turning over a new leaf. Birth is the beginning of new life. Who has ever given birth to themselves? It is amazing how many people think that they will drift into God's presence."

Even Nicodemus couldn't understand this (despite Ezekiel 36). Like most of us, Nicodemus found it easier to understand material rather than spiritual concepts. For J.John, John 3:8 implies that "it is more important to experience new birth than to understand it." We may not understand how the wind works, but we can see its effects. We may not understand the working of God's Spirit in our lives, but we should be able to see the effects. Hence, he concludes, all of us need to be born again.

2. The necessity for Christ's death. Nicodemus is still puzzled. Jesus asserts his authority and proceeds by giving Nicodemus an Old Testament illustration, recounting the incident of the snake in the wilderness (John 3:14). The lesson from this analogy is very clear. There can be no life without death. We cannot be saved from God's judgment unless Jesus Christ was lifted on a cross to take the judgment we deserve. That was what Jesus came to do. "Unless you look at the cross, you haven't got a hope in hell" (see v. 16).

An example of this lesson is Jesus' story of the shepherd and the lost sheep. Shepherds were the butt of jokes in Jesus' day. It is staggering that in this story the shepherd left ninety-nine sheep behind—you should never do that and go off after the missing one! When he found it, he didn't berate it, saying, "You stupid sheep." No, the shepherd picked him up and wrapped him around his neck. Then he went into town and had a party. God's like that, says J.John.

3. The necessity for our response. Only those who believed God's promise and looked to the serpent lived. So it is that only those who believe God's promise and look to the cross will live. J.John speaks of his own response to the Christian message, which came about, in part, as he saw the effect of the gospel on other people. Jesus said that everyone who believes in him will have eternal life (v. 15) and, we are told, "to all who received him, to those who believed in his name, he gave the right to become children of God—children born not of natural descent, nor of human decision or a husband's will, but born of God" (John 1:12-13). "It was not through argument that I became a Christian," said J.John. "It was through observation."

Make a direct appeal and expect a response. J.John devotes nearly ten minutes of a forty-five minute sermon to making a challenging and personal appeal.

First, he encourages the congregation to keep coming to St. Andrew's and observe what is going on there.

Second, he appeals again to his own experience of being born again on February 9, 1975. "I can't remember the day I was born, but there seems to be evidence to suggest it. If it is not possible for you to recall a time, is there any evidence of the new life in you?"

Third, J.John spells out for the congregation the specifics of what a born-again Christian looks like, demonstrating that this is not an isolated truth from one part of the Bible only.

[The first letter of] John says you will believe and want to know Jesus Christ, to apply his teaching; you will want to be known as a Christian; you will have a growing honesty about sin and things that are wrong; you will have amazing assurance that you have been forgiven from things of the past; you will have a desire to be with other Christians; you will have a desire to read the Word of God, the Bible. If you have been born again, you will find that these things will naturally follow.

Do you believe and know Jesus? Are you proud to be known as a Christian? Do you have an assurance that you have been forgiven?

Finally, he recaps, "We live in a changing world, but God hasn't changed, human nature hasn't changed; but if we are to encounter the true and living God, we must change.

"I'm not here because I am paid to do this. I am here because I am utterly convinced of it," he says. J.John concludes by slowly offering a prayer and encouraging individuals to repeat it. "If you haven't become a Christian, or you don't know whether you are a Christian, or you're not sure, then I want you to pray this prayer with me."

LESSONS FOR PREACHERS

- Use (your own) humor. However, don't tell jokes if you are not good at it, and even if you are good at it, use jokes wisely so that they do not distract from the central point. It is worth rehearsing stories, anecdotes and jokes in order that they may be told note free and in a natural way.

- Alliterate wisely. Clever use of alliteration enables the thoughts of the sermon to lodge in the mind. Generally speaking, people will not take written notes when you preach. Sermons need to be structured in such a way that the points are memorable. The use of some of the rhetorical techniques mentioned in chapter one (see pp. 25-26) and in the conclusion see (p. 158) helps this process.

- Preach with specific evangelistic intent. I once heard it said that the regular preacher in a local congregation often claims to be preaching evangelistically every Sunday. In practice, however, this can mean that they do not drive the sermon home and make a direct appeal to be born again, although admittedly this might be inappropriate every Sunday. On the other hand, the itinerant evangelist may make a direct appeal, but will not have the privilege of knowing the congregation well and so needs the local pastor to expound the full breadth of the Bible's teaching on the Christian life. The Tim Keller model of preaching the gospel every Sunday helps to avoid both of these extremes (see chap. 2).

- Appeal to a wide range of authorities. J.John cites the biblical text, doctors of science, historical events, personal correspondence as well as his own experience to substantiate his point. Use these sources as evidence to support the central claims of your sermon.

DAVID COOK

Create Interest; Apply Well

David is a Presbyterian minister and former student of Sydney Missionary and Bible College, Australia, where he later became the principal, serving and shaping it for twenty-five years, until 2011. He has also been the director of SMBC's Centre for Preaching. Before preparing for pastoral ministry, David worked in the economic research department of the Reserve Bank.

The Centre for Preaching is a training initiative which aims to encourage and develop candidates in their conviction of the importance of biblical preaching. Its desire is to see God change lives through preaching, and for a renewed commitment to understanding and adapting the message to an audience.[1]

David and his wife, Maxine, continue to be active in ministry. As part of this, David speaks at Christian conventions throughout Australia and overseas. He and Maxine have five adult children and seven grandchildren.

WHAT MAKES DAVID COOK A GOOD COMMUNICATOR?

David is a very engaging preacher. One striking feature of his sermons is the way he actively works to hold the attention of the congregation, showing resonance through shared human encounter. "Engaging" is how I can best describe this: implying attractiveness and winsomeness, but also including the idea of pledge and contract. The engaging preacher makes the meal enticing and at the same time promises that it will be nourishing. Let's see how David actively seeks to enter the world of the listener before assuming that the listener will enter into the world of his sermon.

David has spoken on more than one occasion about the two greatest needs of pastoral ministry today. First, there is the need for the systematic preaching of the Word of God, and, second, for the systematic visitation of the people of God. Most preachers will affirm the first need. But very often the second falls by the wayside in contemporary pastoral ministry. "If pastors are going to help people to change, they must love them, and you love people by visiting them," says David.[2] In his preaching, the application of the Bible to the real-life circumstances of the hearer is a priority.

David Cook likens preaching to an airplane journey. Most energy and concentration are required at the beginning and the end. The takeoff and the landing are the most dangerous and require the greatest engine thrust. In between, while airborne, the plane may cruise along. In preaching, beginnings and endings matter the most. "Maximum thrust at the beginning; maximum thrust at the end," he says. "From the opening words, your talk must be designed to grip the attention of your audience. Never assume interest. Give time therefore to preparing an introduction that people will find interesting and compelling."[3]

Let's look at several sermons and see how David uses the introduction and the conclusion of his sermons to "get his sermon in the air" and "bring it to a satisfactory landing."[4] Most preachers, of course, do more than one thing well. This is true of David, but he is particularly good at beginnings and endings.

Remember: beginnings and endings matter. David illustrates the principle that beginnings and endings matter. This is not just a concern of pedagogy (teaching) but shows soundness in hermeneutics (interpretation) too. In other words, it could be argued that the Bible itself shows that beginnings and endings matter. Reading Genesis 1–2 and Revelation 21–22, for example, gives a great sense of the entirety of the Bible. The same principle applies to the Psalms, reading Psalm 1 and Psalm 150.

We say, "It's not how you begin but how you end that matters." But in Psalm 1 the psalmist shows that how you begin determines how you end. His solidarity isn't with the wicked, the sinner or the mocker (Psalm 1:1): "But his delight is in the law of the LORD" (Psalm 1:2).

The Psalms finish with Psalm 150: "Praise the Lord." The goal, the testimony of the blessed man, is praise: my lungs, my lips, my limbs. Seven instruments are used to praise him. The words of praise occur thirteen times in six verses: a psalm of praise; praise of Yahweh. There is no true theology without doxology.

The principle from the psalmist is clear. Start with Yahweh and your destiny will be that everything that has breath will praise the Lord. The same could be true for the sermon.

Introduce a single Bible text and return to it at the end. In a sermon to SMBC students at the beginning of the academic year, David posed the question, What is life's purpose?

Introduction. He introduced his answer with the following facts: if you are an Australian male, you will live 25,000 days; if you are female, 30,000.

In the light of your life expectancy, what is it that gets you up in the morning to live any of those days? A Google search of this question reveals a lot of different answers.

The apostle Paul's answer could be taken to be Acts 20:24: "I consider my life worth nothing to me, if only I may finish the race and complete the task the Lord Jesus has given me—the task of testifying to the gospel of God's grace."

There is a principle here: God will bury the messenger but not the message. In Acts 20, Paul mentions eight other people who will take up his pioneer work. This is a good reminder to us that we are not indispensable.

The words used to describe his ministry are teaching, preaching, declaring, testifying and proclaiming (Acts 20:20-21, 24, 25, 27). Paul sums up his ministry as a Bible- and gospel-based ministry.

This introduction set up the focus of the sermon around the single verse in Acts 20:24.

Conclusion. The conclusion of this sermon was an application of this verse to the students' future ministry. "What judgment is upon us if we don't count this ministry as precious?" he says. "You've signed the doctrinal basis of this college. I'd rather give you this statement: Acts 20:24."

He continues, "If, as Karl Marx said, a communist is a dead man on reprieve, how much more so is a Christian? Dietrich Bonhoeffer said, 'When Jesus calls a man, he bids him come and die.'"

"The principle for Paul," David points out, "is self-sacrificial love. This will come to me too as I realize I am redeemed, bought with a price, and that I belong to another. When you become a Gideon [a distributor of New Testaments to hotels], you lose the right to say 'no.' When you become a Christian, you lose the right to say 'no' to the interests of God's grace." David continues:

> You will either go with the gospel or live in sacrificial support of those who go. Paul's commitment transcends his concern for himself. We are surrounded by redeemed people who live for ease or extension. We are to be those who live for the completion of our God-given commission.

David circles around his points of application before bringing the sermon to a conclusion. To extend the airplane analogy, he is seeking for a secure resting place and ensuring that in the final moments the tray tables are stowed away, seat belts are securely fastened and congregation members are receptive. Then he lands.

He concludes with a note that he keeps in his wallet:

> When I reach the end of my days, a moment or two from now, I must look backward on something more meaningful than the pursuit of houses and lands and machines and stock and bonds. Nor is fame of any lasting benefit. I will consider my earthly existence to have been wasted unless I can recall a loving family, a consistent investment in the lives of people and an earnest attempt to serve the God who made me. Nothing else makes much sense.[5]

And then in a last reminder of the central theme of the sermon from Acts 20:24, he says, "I consider my life worth nothing to me, if only I may finish the race and complete the task the Lord Jesus has given me—the task of testifying to the gospel of God's grace."

David spends considerable time on the beginning and ending of the sermon, ensuring that, in the first instance, the context is set; and second, that the message is earthed in the lives of the hearers. Preachers should resist rushing straight into the message without ensuring that the congregation is onboard, and at risk of exhausting the illustration they should not hurry the congregation off the plane before they have collected all their personal belongings and made themselves ready for their onward journey!

Draw people in through a great human-interest story. David preached to Wycliffe Hall students in Oxford on Romans 5:1-11, in part to illustrate the genre of preaching a New Testament letter.

His introduction focused on a trip to the Kruger National Park in South Africa. He had witnessed a herd of elephants from close proximity. A five-ton bull elephant turned around, started flapping its ears, stamped on the ground and appeared to be coming directly toward the group he was with. "My son thought this was wonderful," said David, "but I was petrified. The guard said they were mostly bluffing. Fortunately the guard started the vehicle and then we were safe. But I thought, this is a new experience for me. I have never been charged by a bull elephant in my life. I've seen them in the zoo, at the circus, but not up close."

David's point was that there is a huge contrast between seeing an elephant in the wild and seeing a tame elephant behind bars.

"What I am saying to you today is a tragic truth: that there is an awesome, momentous Christian gospel, but for the majority of Christian people there is a chained counterfeit alternative. How does it happen, that the counterfeit becomes people's experience rather than the genuine article?"

A story such as this brings great empathy. It draws the congregation in and stirs their emotions, enabling them to feel the great contrast between a tame elephant and an elephant in the wild. From this starting point, the preacher can move immediately to outline the contrast between the genuine gospel, with its power to make a difference, and the tame, sanitized and entertaining counterfeit message which many people are hearing.

Ask questions of the passage which the congregation may already be considering. I was curious to know how David would introduce a sermon on Obadiah. This is a prophecy that is likely to challenge the sensibilities of a modern hearer, speaking as it does of judgment and of the deceptiveness of human pride.

He began by pointing out that no one ever does anything from a single motive. Why, as a Christian, am I so self-focused? What stops me apologizing when I know that I should? "Our temper gets us into trouble, but our pride keeps us in trouble," he says.

"Why can I forget so much, but I can't forget that pizza man who ripped me off back in Sydney in 1984? What makes me get hurt? What gives me my reactive, self-protective attitude? What makes me feel superior inside when a Christian brother has fallen? I read the Bible and yet I take delight in evil. Why do I rejoice when my brother mourns, and mourn when my brother rejoices? As Augustine said, 'Why have I become such a problem to myself?'"

The answer, according to Augustine and my own experience, is sin. At the root of sin is pride. Pride is evident in the prophecy of Obadiah.

This sermon introduction addressed contemporary issues that every true Christian has to deal with: the ongoing wrestling with the questions of life, the pride we all experience, the frustration at not being very godly. These are familiar problems for all believers.

Having shown resonance with our common problem, David was then able to demonstrate that the world in which the prophet Obadiah receives his vision is not so different from the world you and I live in today. Moreover, the ancient problem of pride in Obadiah's day is not so different either from the problem of pride in our day.

It is also worth remembering that there is a delicate balance between resonating in such a way that the congregation can feel your empathy and not distracting from allowing the passage to "preach" and diagnose needs. This point is well made by David, writing on using illustration, and reflects his personal attitude: "Illustration must be self-effacing, like John the Baptist, pointing away from [itself] to the truth. It is the truth which must be prominent, not the illustration."[6]

LESSONS FOR PREACHERS

- Some preachers may be inclined to bemoan the fact that nothing interesting or noteworthy ever happens to them. But be genuinely interested in people. My own time with David Cook reminded me that people are not sermon fodder. My son said to David, "You are the coolest man I know" (high praise from an eleven-year-old!). Why? Quite simply because he showed an interest in him and spent time with him.

- Constantly apply the passage to yourself and seek resonances with the world around you. Allow yourself to appear in the sermon, but be self-deprecating. Help people see that you have wrestled with the issues yourself as you have applied the Bible to your own life.

- **Enter the world of the congregation before you seek to draw them** into the world of the text. John Stott's memorable **phrase** "double listening" requires being *both* in the world of **the text** *and* in the world of the hearer. Beginnings and end-**ings** should enter the world of the hearer and set up the pa-**rameters** of the sermon, enabling a bridging between two **worlds.**[7]

8

JOHN ORTBERG

Preach with Spiritual Formation in Mind

❖

John Ortberg studied at Wheaton College and Fuller Theological Seminary. He is the author of several books, including *If You Want to Walk on Water, You've Got to Get Out of the Boat*; *The Life You've Always Wanted: Spiritual Growth for Ordinary People*; *Faith and Doubt*; and *When the Game Is Over, It All Goes Back in the Box*.

Having previously worked on the teaching staff of Willow Creek Community Church in Chicago, he is now senior pastor of Menlo Park Presbyterian Church in California, where he lives with his wife, Nancy. Together they have three children.

WHAT MAKES JOHN ORTBERG A GOOD COMMUNICATOR?

John Ortberg preaches about matters of the heart and believes that spiritual formation is essential to becoming more like Jesus Christ. He assumes that through absorbing the preached Word a person's core ambitions and thoughts will become more God-focused. As a result, Christian character will be formed.

In order for this to happen, the right kind of preaching needs to take place. At the National Pastors' Conference in 2007, Ortberg listed the "Ten Deadly Sins of Preaching": the temptation to be inauthentic, the temptation to live for recognition, the temptation to fear, the temptation to comparison, the temptation to exaggerate, the temptation to feel chronically inadequate, the temptation to pride, the temptation to manipulate, the temptation to envy and the temptation to anger.[1]

In *Leadership* magazine, John Ortberg shares this important observation:

> I once was part of a survey on spiritual formation. Thousands of people were asked when they had grown most spiritually, and what had contributed to their growth. The response was humbling—at least for someone who works at a church.[2]

He goes on to state that the main contributor to spiritual growth was not transformational teaching. It was not being part of a small group. It was not reading deep theological books. It was not energetic worship experiences or finding meaningful ways to serve. The surprising conclusion was that suffering is the key to spiritual growth.

Respondents noticed that they grew more during times of loss, pain and crisis than they had done at any other time. "I immediately realized that, as a church, we had not even put anybody in charge of pain distribution!" said John, "So now we are figuring out how to create more pain per attender for maximum spiritual growth!"

But, he notes, the process is not automatic. Suffering does not automatically foster spiritual growth. In fact, "if we have not thought carefully about the intersection of crisis and ministry, then we may have neglected the most soul-formative moments that occur in the lives of our people."

For those of us involved in theological education, the term *spiritual formation* is important, but the phrase itself is slippery. I am intrigued to discover what spiritual formation means for John Ortberg.[3]

In this chapter we will focus on two sermons. The first was preached on Easter Sunday, from Mark 16:1-8. Here John seeks to persuade the congregation of the significance of the resurrection. The second sermon was preached at the start of a new series on key words in the Bible. Here he examines the word *redemption*, from an overview of Genesis 1:1–11:4.

SERMON ONE: PREACHING THE RESURRECTION

As he opens his sermon, without story or anecdote, John cuts straight to the ending of Mark's Gospel, acknowledging that this is a less familiar resurrection account.

Help the congregation stay with you. John helps the congregation stay with him by asking a number of questions of the text of the Gospels, for example, "Why would it have been written like that?"

He also anticipates the kinds of questions the congregation may have in mind, for example when he says such things as, "And often the thinking kind of goes like this . . ."; "Keep that in mind and we'll come back to this"; or "Now some people think . . ."

He anticipates some reaction from the congregation, mirroring Mary's concerns as she stood at the mouth of the empty tomb: "Maybe you lack information, and you need to decide, 'I'm going to learn more,' but [Mary] realized for her that this wasn't her deal. Her issue was a commitment deal, that she was just in kind of spiritual drift mode. . . . Have you ever taken that step? If you haven't, what a great day to do it!"

He also teases out the implications of these questions for the hearers: "When it first happened, when the tomb was empty, these women knew it was a fact, but it actually took a while for them to understand that it was good news."

> So what I'd like to do in this talk is to try to help us see what happened through their eyes. Everybody here knows we're here because of Easter, but many . . . maybe most people . . . don't really understand there is a back story to this idea of resurrection that is critical to understanding Easter, and it's actually a really powerful reason for understanding that this resurrection of Jesus really did happen.

His conclusion is that Jesus came into a world that had expectations of the resurrection, but would not have anticipated the personal individual resurrection to happen in the way that it did.

Find illustrations that resonate and help you reinforce your point. The first illustration was taken from the film *The Sixth Sense*, starring Bruce Willis. It was helpful because of the clever way the child actor said, "I see dead people," but only later on do we realize that we, the audience, are viewing death from a surprising and skewed perspective.

John's humor and self-deprecation also come across:

> And when they really get scared, they reach over and bend your finger . . . one single finger . . . backwards, like the more pain they inflict on you the better they feel. And the tension got so bad, finally Nancy said to me, "John, if you

won't let go of my finger, I'm changing seats." . . . Because there is no fear like death.

Second, John spoke about resurrection as a team event using a baseball analogy: "Resurrection was not a private event. It was a team sport." Just as in baseball, the team wins, not just the individual. So it was assumed that when resurrection happened it would be for all believers, not just an individual:

> But now, because of this, nobody in Israel would ever think to claim that one individual had been resurrected in the middle of history. If somebody were to claim that, then the response would have been: "Has disease been eradicated? Has justice broken out? Has suffering ended? Stop talking nonsense." It would be kind of like . . . I'm from Chicago originally. We believe one day the Cubs will win the World Series, and then history will come to an end. But nobody would say, "This year just the Cubs first baseman will win the World Series. The rest of the team will have to wait." That wouldn't make any sense at all. The World Series is a team deal. Resurrection was understood to be a team deal.

Third, he told a familiar joke about a neighbor's dead rabbit apparently coming back to life. In the joke, a woman noticed her dog running around with the neighbor's dead rabbit in its mouth. Embarrassed by her dog's behavior, she bought a replacement and put it in the cage. This caused huge shock to the neighbor, because apparently the rabbit had died the previous day and been buried in the garden, and the dog had dug it up. It ended with the clever line: "People in the ancient world knew dead rabbits tend to stay dead. They also knew dead rabbis tend to stay dead." He backed this up by quoting from Tom Wright: "There were many messianic movements in the first century. In every case, the would-be Messiah got crucified by Rome, as Jesus did." And this is what he writes: "In not one single case do we hear the slightest mention of the disappointed followers claiming their hero had been raised from the dead. They knew better."

Make good use of apologetic arguments. John makes use of arguments in several ways. To some he says, "Maybe you lack information, and you need to decide"; others he encourages, not just to understand the truth but also to appreciate its personal significance, and their need to cross over the line from unbelief to faith.

One of the unique aspects of Christianity compared to any other faith or movement is that it actually traces its origin to one particular event in one moment on one day in history. This is not true for Buddhism or Judaism or Islam or atheism.

He mentions the four biographies of Jesus in the New Testament: Matthew, Mark, Luke and John, noting that most of the Gospels are devoted to the last week in Jesus' life.

There are two surprises at the end of Mark 16. First, the tomb was empty: "He is not here. See the place where they laid him." Second, Jesus appeared to his followers. "He is going ahead of you into Galilee. There you will see him, just as he told you."

He speaks about the evidence for the empty tomb and the actual sightings of the resurrected Jesus. He concludes: "It was the combination of these two factors together that was overwhelming."

John goes on to list the "reasons [why] it was not a made-up story." He also seeks to anticipate potential objections with phrases such as: "Often the thinking goes like this . . . ," refuting what C. S. Lewis summarized as "chronological snobbery" (ancient people were gullible; we are not).

He plants thoughts and then comes back to develop them later. In this sermon he does this with the illustration taken from *The Sixth Sense*, from which the phrase "I see dead people" is quoted. He returns to it later in order to link the arguments for the resurrection with the need to "cross the line" into a new relationship with the resurrected Jesus.

Make personal application. "Here is where it gets personal. There is one more step, and it's a step for you." John argues that the resurrection is not just good news but true news. Jesus said, "Whoever lives and believes in me will never die" (John 11:26).

> That is not a metaphor. That is not a vague hope. It's like you're going to slip under that surface, and then those big arms are going to grab you, and death itself no longer has power. Now either that is true or it's not, but don't just go through your life with this kind of vague drifting. . . . Death has no power to take you from the arms of the Father. Guilt cannot separate you from God. Whatever bad news you face, if you have crossed that line, if you have trusted this man Jesus, you have a resurrection coming.

He takes time to list the challenges faced by different members of the congregation: the elderly, husbands and wives, young people, addicts, and so forth. He also speaks to their felt needs and their real needs: health, devastation, fear, anxiety and guilt.

> You, elderly person, whose health is so frail, so fragile, almost gone, you don't have to live in fear. You have a resurrection coming. You, devastated husband, whose wife has left you, and you feel so betrayed and so alone, you don't have to live like a loser. You have a resurrection com-

ing. You, frightened parents of a depressed child, you don't have to live burdened by this weight of blame. You have a resurrection coming. An anxious worker out of a job, out of money, a guilt-ridden addict hiding in the shadows, a lonely young person longing to be loved, if you have taken this step, if you have given the leadership of your life to Jesus Christ, you are living in a new reality. Those arms are plenty strong enough.

SERMON TWO: PREACHING REDEMPTION

I have particularly selected this sermon to gain a sense of what John means by the term *spiritual formation*. We have already noted that this phrase seems to defy precise definition. What does it mean to be "formed" and to be formed "spiritually"?

Tell the big Bible story in a way that relates to the audience's own story. What I appreciate about John's preaching is that there are no "top ten tips" for improving your Christian well-being. Rather, John is keen that the grand story of the Bible affects the narrative for each individual Christian. Scripture should shape the Christian's script. This second sermon demonstrates how John does this.

Picking up on a quote from R. C. Sproul, John argues that the most important question human beings can ask is: "What is God like?"

In Genesis we find answers to this. There is a pattern: God reveals himself to human beings, people "mess it up," and God comes in and redeems it.

This sermon is the first in a series on key words in the Bible. Here in "Redemption" he speaks in general terms, giving a big-sweep "walk through" of the first eleven chapters of Genesis.

96

God is setting the stage for his future, promised redemption.

Despite the magnitude of the themes, John will still make comments such as: "Note the tender detail here" and "Another redemptive note from God."

With respect to Adam and Eve, God not only promises redemption through their offspring but also clothes them so that they may come into his presence without shame. This also anticipates the fact that innocent blood is shed so that shame may be covered. "Redemption comes at a cost," he says.

In the case of Cain, the "mark [of Cain]" (see Genesis 4:15) implies that God works to bring something good out of something very bad.

From Genesis 6, John argues, we get a sense of the heart of God as "one who loves every human being way more than you and I do from the beginning of time, and whose heart is broken by everyone who goes off down a wrong, self-destructive path. How much pain must be in the heart of God? I cannot even imagine what it must be like to be God."

God sends a flood, but he begins again with a man named Noah. Things continue to get worse (see Genesis 11). Man will seek to make a name for himself. "We will be like God," they reason. God comes down. He restrains them so that they won't destroy themselves.

John encourages us to note the pattern of a "fall," which is followed by God acting redemptively. This pattern is repeated throughout the first eleven chapters of Genesis. However, this should all be viewed as a prologue to Genesis 12.

Here God promises that he will take a very ordinary man (Abram), give him a new name and start a new people. God is a redeemer of the human race, later promising to Moses, "I will free you . . . redeem you. . . . I will take you as my own people and . . . be your God" (Exodus 6:6-7). Job makes precisely this point: "I know that my Redeemer lives" (Job 19:25).

The retelling of this grand sweep of the first eleven chapters of Genesis helps the audience to connect the ancient story with the day-to-day script of their own lives. We share with them the pattern of "fall," but we may also experience God's redemptive hand. It takes time to be immersed into God's big story line, so a sermon such as this one takes trouble to retell it carefully.

Identify with and recognize "the mess" of our lives. "We all find ourselves in this place where life is not turning out the way we had anticipated," says John. "It's kind of a mess, and we don't know how to fix it up. Is there somebody out there who can come and is willing to pay the price to straighten things out?"

He endorses this by saying that the primary need of Christians is a true knowledge of God. This knowledge includes the fact that he is the kind of God who comes alongside us when we are in a mess and does something redemptive. This reinforces the opening quotation from R. C. Sproul that the greatest human need is to understand the true identity of God. The God we worship is a God who redeems.

Use illustrations that connect at the level of the affections. The illustrations in this sermon were not primarily designed to assist understanding, rather they work at the level of the affections, connecting with the human heart and, in some cases, eliciting emotional reactions.

1. Piano playing. Here John tells the story of a nine-year-old boy sneaking on stage and playing "Chopsticks" on the grand piano before the Polish concert pianist Ignacy Jan Paderewski appeared for his concert performance. To the audience's surprise the maestro came alongside the young boy and improvised with him. This illustration was enacted on the stage next to John as he told it.

He made the following analogy: we are like the nine-year-old boy playing "Chopsticks"; God the maestro comes alongside to make our "mess" into a beautiful tune. The point is powerfully, visually and audibly reinforced.

2. *Redemption stamps.* John asked the congregation, "What was the biggest publication in the 1960s?" It was the *S&H* catalog, which operated a redemption center for those who had collected enough Green Stamps.

The analogy is that in the same way that Green Stamps could be redeemed for something wonderful, God is still in the redemption business.

> With endless patience and with infinite cost to himself . . . God has been waiting since the beginning of history until one day at the fullness of time there came a Son of Eve. God sent him to a redemption center. Only one item in his catalog: "I want one of you."

The cross is God's redemption center.

3. *Schindler's List.* The illustration of the redemption center leads into a final, powerful and emotional illustration taken from the movie *Schindler's List.*

All the threads of the sermon on the theme of redemption are woven together in a great climax in this film clip. Schindler chides himself that he could have done more; he could have sold more goods and redeemed more people from captivity. But Stern reminds him that through his sacrificial actions many people were already redeemed and set free for a new life.

There is a redemption center, and so God says now what he has been saying to the human race for so long, "Why don't you just come on into the redemption center? Why don't you trade that old guilt . . . it's not getting you anywhere . . . for a little forgiveness? Why don't you trade your old sinful life, which will never get you what you want, for a redeemed life? Why don't you trade your regret for some hope? Why don't you trade your despair for some faith? Why don't you trade that human inadequacy for some power God will give you?"

Why would God do this? Why would God make a trade like that? Because Somebody paid a price. Because there is a Redeemer. Because the story of the world we can barely allow ourselves to hope might be true is the story of a God who is a redeeming God who takes messes in people's lives and stuff that's shattered and stuff that's broken and stuff that nobody can fix. God says, "You bring it to Me. You bring it to the redemption center, and I'll redeem it. I paid a price, that's who I have been from all eternity, and I'm still in the redeeming business." That's our God. That's our God.

John acknowledges the huge mess in our world. But at the same time this is a powerful reminder that the story of the Bible is like no other story on earth—it is the story of redemption in which God paid the ultimate price to redeem us. God offers an amazing trade-in: our old life for his new life, and God is still in the redeeming business.

CONCLUSION

Prior to writing this chapter, I had read John Ortberg's books but had not heard him preach. I was quite surprised to discover that his preaching was quite monosyllabic. He uses what would appear to be a full script, and, in fact, the content of the sermon could easily be turned directly into a script for a book.

Having said that, his sermons are very compelling and easy to listen to. He is a great wordsmith. He communicates Christian truth in an exceptionally engaging way through his simple storytelling and humanity. His humor reveals a willingness to mock his own shortfalls, and his sermons resonate with the ordinariness of human conversations: taking his children swimming, going to a concert, watching a movie and so forth.

HOW DOES JOHN ORTBERG THINK SPIRITUAL FORMATION HAPPENS?

I have chosen John Ortberg for inclusion in this selection of fine preachers in part because of his emphasis on spiritual formation. How, I wonder, does he believe this happens?

Among the many things alluded to in the previous sermons, I suggest at least the following takes place in his preaching.

First, spiritual formation flows from a true knowledge of God and subsequently a true knowledge of ourselves. Christlike character comes about only when we are deeply immersed in God's big story and dragged into that narrative.

It strikes me that this is not so different from the goals of John Calvin as outlined in *Institutes of the Christian Religion*. Here Calvin spent two thousand pages exploring the doctrine of the knowledge of God (Creator and Redeemer), which in turn leads to the doctrine of the knowledge of ourselves.[5]

Second, spiritual formation takes time. As John says in "Don't Waste a Crisis": "Speed may be good when it comes to ambulances and Internet connections—maybe even when it comes to the length of sermons, if my wife can be trusted—

but all the technology at MIT cannot microwave the healing of a human heart.[6]

John's preaching is measured and careful. One also gets the sense that there is "joined-up thinking," and the hearer wants to hang around for the next sermon in order to imbibe the contents of the Bible story and drink deeply.

LESSONS FOR PREACHERS

- Don't feel as though you have to say everything every time you stand up to preach. God's story is a big story, and its full explanation requires a lifetime.

- Connect with the human heart in all its joys and sufferings, and bring people to God's redemption center: the cross.

- Use simple, clear illustrations and make use of the arts (movies, music, etc.) if they can help you to amplify or apply your point well.

- Anticipate and answer people's objections. Ensure that the questions you ask (and answer) really are people's questions. Then help them to see how the Bible has provided a thorough response.

9

NICKY GUMBEL

Make Much of Jesus Christ

Nicky Gumbel trained for ministry at Wycliffe Hall, Oxford, having first completed a law degree at Cambridge University, followed by six years of practicing as a barrister (lawyer). From Wycliffe, he became curate at Holy Trinity Brompton and succeeded Sandy Millar as the vicar. He is married to Pippa, and they have three children.

Nicky is best known as the chief promoter of the Alpha Course.[1] The growth of Alpha is nothing short of a phenomenon in the life of the church, with estimates of 16.5 million people having attended the course in 169 countries.

Most of the topics Nicky speaks on are how-to talks, such as "how to love your enemies" and "how to pray." His Alpha talks take forty minutes and are thematic, covering the basics of the Christian faith. Says Nicky,

> I found this thing that . . . had this appeal to people outside of the Church, and we've been trying to work out why this is ever since. We've got something that works in practice,

and we're trying to work out how we can make it work in theory. So, why is it? I think there are a number of things about it. I think it's a low-key, relaxed, unthreatening, non-confrontational way for people to explore pretty big questions. I think a lot of people do have questions about life, "What's the purpose of my life?," "What's the meaning of my life?," "Why am I here?" . . . It's hard to find a place where you can discuss those issues. You can't go down to the pub and say, "What do you think the meaning of life is?" It's hard at a football match to discuss those kinds of issues. But actually, most people have those questions, somewhere in the back of their minds. And if you can find a place where you can discuss them with a group of people who, like you, are outside of the Church, and it's a non-threatening, relaxed environment, quite a lot of people want to do that.[2]

Perhaps it is because the Christian faith is conveyed in a non-threatening and disarming way that Alpha has been a hugely successful evangelistic tool. However, Nicky resists using the term *evangelical* to describe himself out of a dislike for any labels. He is a Christian first and an Anglican second. He is a very Jesus-centered person: "I'm not really committed to Alpha at all. I'm a Christian. I'm committed to Jesus Christ and I want people to know about Christ, because it's the most wonderful thing."[3] That statement shapes the focus of his preaching.

WHAT MAKES NICKY GUMBEL A GOOD COMMUNICATOR?

The sermon that we are going to look at was advertised as part of "Vision Sunday" and preached on January 31, 2010.[4] The Bible text was Matthew 9:36-38.

Start in the world and begin with felt needs. This sermon did not begin with an announcement of the text. In fact, we were eight minutes into a thirty-five-minute sermon before we got to Matthew 9. Nicky spent the first quarter of the sermon ensuring that his congregation sensed the need for his topic. Also, his vision extended beyond an assumption of interest from the church congregation and addressed concerns in the minds of the wider nonchurched audience. He assumed that in a congregation of nearly a thousand people many of those present were visitors or first-timers.

First, he spoke about a lunch meeting he had had with the editor of a national newspaper. He said that he had asked him about the newspaper's coverage of Christian/church stories. This editor had implied that "the media regards the church as an irrelevance." He concluded, "This is a chilling statement."

Then he went on to paint a picture of today's church, as seen through the eyes of the media. They see declining numbers. On the one hand, attendance is going down, and the average age is going up. The church is in financial meltdown, and the media are witnessing the closing-down sale of the Church of England. On the other hand, they are seeing the implications of the church's demise in society, such as in the violence of children to children.

From these two opening remarks, Nicky begins to address one of the key ways in which the church can, and should, address issues that matter to national newspaper editors:

> Look at parenting . . . family life really does matter. It does matter whether or not people marry. Only 3% of unmarried couples stay together until their child is fifteen years old. But that is not what people think.

He said that 45 percent of the population agree that it makes no difference whether people are married or not. However, 60 percent of couples with fifteen-year-old children have stayed together, and 90 percent of these couples are married ones.

Nicky ensures that he has gained a hearing with the congregation before bringing them to his Bible text.

Speak to society's needs. Nicky begins by acknowledging common personal needs, such as loneliness and directionless living. He turns to national needs, such as the need for change and reformation in society. He comments from newspaper articles on perceptions of the state of the nation.

He also comments on what he perceives to be urgent global needs, citing as an example the situation in Haiti. He points out that an earthquake of the same magnitude as the one that hit Haiti on January 12, 2010 (7.0 magnitude) also hit Los Angeles. The effect of the LA earthquake was that sixty people, not 200,000, died. The reason for this huge difference was because Californian buildings were properly built, and the people were not living in poverty.

So his sermon touches on the needs of today, not just at a personal level but nationally and globally as well.

Link your general remarks to the specific theme of the sermon. Nicky reminds the congregation that although they may feel depressed by the trends within society, we have been here before. This is not the first time in history that society has faced such depressing scenarios.

The media looks at the downward trend and assumes that it will continue to go in this direction. But this is not necessarily the case. Go back in history: it's not like that.

In 1780, church-going declined to almost zero. There was

drinking, gambling and prostitution—not so different from our own day. But "there were people around who said, 'This will not do. This society needs Jesus.' A Wesley arose, a Whitfield, a Wilberforce, and Robert Raikes who saw 300,000 coming to Sunday schools: virtually every child had a chance to hear about Jesus."

When comparing the current state of society with that of two hundred years ago, Nicky asks, Could it change for us today? The answer, he says, is not to go back two hundred years, but rather to go back two thousand years.

How did Jesus cause change? He mobilized people. Matthew 9 contains "absolutely critical verses," the lynchpin in Matthew's Gospel.

Build your case around cumulative points. Nicky does not just make "preachers' points." Rather, the four main topics of the sermon build one upon another.

1. The need is urgent. Matthew 9:36 provides a good description of so many people in life today: weary, confused, helpless (the Greek means, "thrown away"). Up till now we've been throwing things away; now we're throwing people away. People desperately need Jesus.

Nicky says, "Something has gone wrong with our society. . . . We have lost Jesus Christ . . . because we have lost community and mutual dependence." The need is urgent, not just personally, but in order to mend society too.

2. The motive is love. Nicky offers another definition of a Greek word, often translated as "compassion" in English, but coming from the word to describe our "guts"; that is, from our innermost being.

Compassion drives change: it comes from Jesus, from his

heart. So, "you have God's heart, you have the compassion of Jesus, because the Spirit of Jesus is living in you and that is all that you need to change the world. . . . Every single one of you: you are responsible for changing the world."

Nicky quotes and summarizes from some observations about larger churches by former Holy Trinity Brompton rector John Collins. He makes his own application to HTB today. John Collins listed the advantages of being a larger church, and the vulnerabilities of the larger church (passivity being the main one).

Nicky applies John Collins's notes to three particular challenges for the congregation:

> Myth 1—HTB has a large staff, therefore I'm not needed; myth 2—There's someone else who's better qualified and has more time; myth 3—They don't need me, someone else will do it. But God has given to you a unique calling . . . to change the world.

3. *The trigger is prayer.* Jesus said, "Ask the Lord to send workers." Nicky points to a visual description of the church's vision for that year, showing that the base is made up of prayer and worship. "This is not a business," he says; rather, the church grows only through prayer and worship.

4. *The potential is vast.* The harvest is plentiful, but the workers are few. Nicky invites the congregation to

> think of the church declining, declining . . . but then think of Gideon. You don't need all those people; you only need three hundred committed people. Even thirty years ago people came to church because it was expected. But [today] if you come to church, you are already making a stand.

This is not the moment to defend our institutions, but it is time for us to go on the attack, and you can do it because you have the Spirit of Christ living in you and you can change the world.

Nicky motivates and mobilizes every individual in this large congregation.

Use statistics and quotes to build your case. Nicky trained as a lawyer, and while listening to him preach you feel as though he is using evidence to build up his case for Jesus Christ. He quotes from a wide range of sources, including a pop star, a *Times of London* journalist, a world-renowned chess player and author, politicians, theologians, and a veteran preacher. Here are some examples.

Nicky uses the Lily Allen song "22" to identify with the young majority in the congregation, illustrating the way that hopes and dreams may quickly pass you by. He also cites an article by Rosemary Bennett and Mary Bowers in the *Times*, "Loneliness: The Silent Epidemic Sweeping Through Britain."[5] Nicky concludes that we throw away our old people, but it's not just old people who are lonely; the same is true of many young people too.

Nicky speaks of a memorable visit he and his wife, Pippa, paid to the late John Stott, who, then at the age of eighty-four, shared his anxieties about loneliness following a fall which resulted in his breaking his hip. He then read an extended quote from John Stott's last book, *The Radical Disciple*, on the subject of recovering a sense of the dignity of dependence.

Throughout the sermon, Nicky also cited a large number of statistics, some from formal sources and some anecdotal, including:

* 11 percent of people over sixty-five feel lonely all the time

- 21 percent of eighteen- to twenty-four year olds said loneliness was one of their main concerns

- a pastor in Sheffield said that out of 1.5 million people, only 0.9 percent go to church

- the only area of church life which is growing in Britain is among the eighty to eighty-nine-year age group

He refers to HTB courses for overcoming addictions, courses on depression, money, marriage and parenting, and caring for ex-offenders. All the time he uses facts to demonstrate that everyone needs Jesus.

Keep talking about Jesus Christ. What comes across strongly in the sermon is that the Christ of Christianity is the focus of Nicky's preaching. Indeed, I noted the number of times he spoke about the need for Jesus:

- He repeats the phrase "people desperately need Jesus" (in their desperate loneliness).

- We have lost Jesus Christ, he says, because we have lost community and mutual dependence.

- He says, "Supremely, people need Jesus."

- "As the Spirit of Christ lives in you," he says, "you can change the world."

Nicky's argument is that Jesus Christ remains attractive and unites believers, while other things bring division. So, preach Jesus! At the end, the congregation is left with the abiding impression that this preacher is passionate about Jesus Christ.

LESSONS FOR PREACHERS

- Speak to the felt needs of the wider society. It is easy to dismiss preaching to such needs on the grounds that these are not synonymous with real needs. However, Nicky carefully moves from empathy over issues of loneliness and a sense of lostness—common across much of modern society—to speak about how Jesus meets our real needs. We need to start where people are at.[6]

• Paint a big vision for God's church. Holy Trinity Brompton has one of the largest church attendances in England, and with its strong identification with Alpha there is a sense in which its reach is global. However, all preachers, even in more humble settings, should have a vision for a Jesus-centered transformation, first of individuals, then of the church community and then outward to the wider world. For, without this vision, churches remain parochial and congregations wither and die.

• People were amazed at Jesus' teaching, his understanding and his answers (Matthew 7:28-29; Luke 2:47). The common people heard him gladly (Mark 12:37). Our preaching should be all about Jesus Christ. Yes, there is a place for talking about a denomination, church government, ethical issues, and indeed "the whole counsel of God." But, along with the apostle Paul, we should resolve to "know nothing . . . except Jesus Christ and him crucified" (1 Corinthians 2:2).

10

Preach with Urgency and Evangelistic Zeal

❖

Rico Tice has been associate minister at All Souls Church, Langham Place, London, since 1994. He is the coauthor of the inquirers' course *Christianity Explored*, and is regularly involved in evangelistic events around the United Kingdom. He also presents the DVD talks for *Christianity Explored*. He is married to Lucy, and they have one son, Peter. Rico maintains his interest in Christians in sport, with a particular love for rugby and golf.

Watching his grandmother die had a profound effect on him and precipitated his passion to make the gospel of Jesus Christ known with a sense of urgency:

> I left her in God's hands but I came out thinking, "Rico, if you really believe the gospel to be true, if the cross is God's escape route from hell to heaven, and you love people, then the priority in your life will be to tell them and warn them." This caused me to see that my focus had to be evangelism. . . . There is that feeling in your heart of bleeding for the lost—the sense of being in debt to them—and I think this is fundamental to an evangelist's mentality.[1]

Over the years *Christianity Explored* has been taught and honed into a widely used and effective evangelistic tool. Two features of the course are significant. The first is that participants read the Gospel of Mark for themselves over the first seven weeks, in order, as Rico says, that they may "meet the person of Jesus Christ as he walks off the pages of the Bible." The talks are designed to enthuse hearers to discover Jesus for themselves from their own reading of Mark's Gospel.[2] Second, the course is direct in pointing out the cost of following Jesus Christ as one of his disciples. Rico speaks straight at the camera, whether he is watching rugby training or walking around Chatham Dockyard. He speaks plainly about hell and reminds participants that becoming a Christian is not a soft option. This theme is evident in the sermon we shall look at.

In his commendation of the *Christianity Explored* course on its website, Michael Horton states: "Combining evangelistic passion and evangelical commitments, one need not choose between relevance and faithfulness."[3]

Key features of the course include anticipating answers to the following questions: If you could ask God one question, what would it be? Seventy or eighty percent of people believe God is there, but how can we relate to him? There are also responses to questions like: Who is Jesus? Why did he die? And how may I follow him?

The desire to ask hard questions and yet still communicate in a popular and accessible way is a key feature both of the course and of Rico's preaching.

WHAT MAKES RICO TICE A GOOD COMMUNICATOR?

Rico's sermon was preached at All Souls Church on Sunday,

August 22, 2010, in a series called "Faith's National Portrait Gallery."

The text was from Hebrews 11:32-40 and titled, "Faith That Looks Forward to What Is Promised."

Speak with passion. Although Rico writes out his sermons word for word, they do not give the impression of having been carefully scripted. Many of the points are clipped, staccato sentences. But it feels very fresh; Rico owns the message. Everything he says has a personal and an urgent tone. However, this does not mean that the sermon is about him. Rather, his passion is that his audience might grasp the significance of the message, something which comes through very strongly.

Let your sermon structure serve you. The structure of this sermon is:

• In the Christian life, finishing is everything.

• Not finishing is a real risk.

• The key to finishing is faith.

Rico claims, "This is a one-word sermon: the driving point in the two lists is 'others.'" In Hebrews 11:35, *others* "'were tortured and refused to be released' in order to obtain a better resurrection." The question he asks is: Are you among those "others"?

There is an underlying structure, but it is not "tight" or particularly methodical. Rico uses a broad outline, and this enables him to unleash his passionate desire to persuade you of the truth of what he believes.

Set your sermon in the broader context of the sermon series. Previous sermons in this series had covered the exciting victories of the men and women of faith (Hebrews 11:1-35). This sermon deals with the enduring virtues of faith (vv. 35-38).

Rico asserts: "Having true faith in God is no assurance of comfort in this life. There is a heretical teaching which promises a prosperity gospel."

The "others" listed faced jeers and flogging, being chained and put in prison. They were stoned, sawn in two, killed by the sword; they were destitute, persecuted and mistreated (see Hebrews 11:36-37). The clear challenge is whether we will allow ourselves to be numbered among them.

Illustrate continually. Rico uses three main illustrations of suffering. He tells of a couple in the congregation where the husband is serving his wife, who has had a stroke. He refers to the Maccabean martyrs.[4] His particular focus is on the mother's encouragement to each of the seven brothers who are murdered one by one, leaving her still living. He concludes: "I don't apologize for this gruesome illustration." Our attempt to live "designer lives" contrasts greatly with what Christians have had to suffer in the past.

Third, he uses the illustration of this life being like a journey to our heavenly home: "I have the title deeds to the house, but I haven't yet moved in." We should all live our lives in this expectation.

Recount self-deprecating stories that enable the hearer to grasp the reality of following Jesus. In all of Rico's sermons, the listener gets the firm impression that eternity is at stake. However, one thing that rescues this approach from the caricature of the Bible-thumping "turn-or-burn" evangelist is the way he humbly points to his own weaknesses in seeking to live out the Christian life.

A good example of this is the "bleep test" story recounted in his *Christianity Explored* talk "Jesus—His Aim."[5] Rico speaks about the agony of going through a bleep test, and the indignity and physical sickness that resulted. This is used to illustrate how hard it is to pass such a rigorous physical fitness test, and how humiliating it is if we fail to prepare properly for it. "Listening to what Jesus has to say about you and me is like going through fitness tests. It means being told what we are really like beneath the surface, and it is a very uncomfortable experience."[6]

Because Rico has been self-deprecating about his own physical fitness failures, he breaks down our defenses, thereby enabling us to hear challenging words about Jesus' demand on our lives.

Use urgent language. The following quotes show how the urgency of the message comes across.

> "Here is the issue: There is a massive danger that my faith and trust in Christ ends halfway through."

> Commenting on Hebrews 3:7-8: "So, as the Holy Spirit says: 'Today, if you hear his voice, do not harden your hearts as you did in the rebellion, during the time of testing in the desert,' " Rico says, "If you can't get this into your head, to quote Tim Keller, you are doomed."

> "I want to weep when I think of this. We can throw this away."

Clearly there is no point in saying the latter if it is not true, but if it is true, as it is for Rico, then it will have a powerful impact on the congregation. Rico's urgency affects the congregation: they must not remain indifferent.

Apply the same sense of urgency to Christian and non-Christian alike. Non-Christian. As an aside, Rico says, "If you're not a

Christian here, thanks for coming. There are some things you need to know about being a Christian."

He then gives a short summary of what it means to be a Christian. There is a need for information—the facts about Christianity. There is a need for trust and faith. Plus you need to assent and be convicted that the information is true: Jesus died that I might be able to be forgiven on the Day of Judgment. "There are lots of people who have the information. They assent to it, but they live their own lives," he says.

Rico makes the assumption that there are non-Christians present, and so, even though his primary audience is the All Souls congregation, he also applies the message to those who are not Christians as he goes along.

There are sentiments that Rico regularly repeats in his sermons and during the *Christianity Explored* course: "You are more sinful than you might ever imagine, but more loved than you could ever dream." Such words enable him to do a very similar thing to what Tim Keller does, namely, to preach the gospel to a mixed audience on every occasion.

Christian. Commenting on the heroes of Hebrews 11, Rico says: "We love these stories of faith because we love success." The danger for Christians, though, is that our faith is not in God but in our agenda for God. People say, "I trusted God, and he didn't come through for me."

> There is a danger when the good thing becomes a God thing: we say, "Where is the house I wanted, the job I wanted, the husband I wanted, the wife I wanted, and the children I wanted?" Our hearts get kidnapped. . . . We rail at God, saying, "Why did I not get my agenda?" . . . Are we faithful in the midst of our difficulties?

117

Do the work of an evangelist (2 Timothy 4:5). In a YouTube clip, Rico talks about evangelism:

Everyone has to pay for their sin unless it is paid for at the cross. If you believe the cross was so important that it's the only place I can get my sin paid for in death and blood, then you'll see that evangelism is the priority in our lives.[7]

Rico argues that his experience of preaching is that the best spontaneity is rehearsed. He trains himself to keep telling "the tough truths" and works hard to try to speak naturally and faithfully of Jesus Christ. If he can do that part, God will do his job of opening blind eyes.

His huge motivation is Romans 1:14, where Paul writes: "I am obligated both to Greeks and non-Greeks, both to the wise and the foolish." "Consequently," says Rico, "I am in debt to God until I have passed the gospel on to others. On Judgment Day others will look across to me and say: Why didn't you tell me?"

LESSONS FOR PREACHERS

- Allow your vulnerability to show in order that the congregation may conclude, "If this gospel works even for you, then it should work for me too."

- Be passionate and urgent. You can't fake it, but if you feel it, don't be afraid to show it. The old African American pattern for preaching preparation holds true: "Pray myself hot; read myself full; let myself loose!"

- Evangelize all the time. Even if you are speaking to the regular congregation, always bear in mind that there will be visitors present, and take the opportunity to tell them about Jesus Christ.

11

ALISTAIR BEGG

Persuade People by
Passionate Argument from the Bible

Alistair Begg has been in pastoral ministry since 1975. Following graduation from the London School of Theology, he served eight years in Scotland, both at Charlotte Chapel in Edinburgh and Hamilton Baptist Church, near Glasgow. He took up the post of senior pastor at Parkside Church in suburban Cleveland, Ohio, where he has worked since 1983.

As well as being the principal preacher at Parkside, Alistair has played an active part in enabling a succession of young men to take up preaching throughout the United States. His teaching is heard daily across the nation on over a thousand radio stations that air the program *Truth for Life*. He has written a number of books, including *The Hand of God* and a revision of Spurgeon's devotional *Morning and Evening*. He has been married to Susan for thirty-four years, and they are the parents of three adult children, and now grandparents.

Alistair regularly preaches in the United Kingdom. In 2010

he gave the Bible readings at Bible by the Beach in Eastbourne and at Keswick Convention in Cumbria, England.

WHAT MAKES ALISTAIR BEGG A GOOD COMMUNICATOR?

The following observations are taken primarily from a sermon preached on January 10, 2010, at Parkside Church, based on 1 Peter 2:4-9, and set in the context of priorities for the church for the year ahead.

Take a single text, and expound, apply and lodge it in people's minds. Peter uses Old Testament temple language and applies it to the New Testament people of God. One single phrase, "declare the praises of him" (1 Peter 2:9), summarizes the theme of the sermon.

This was a message for Parkside as they began the New Year. It was a sermon that helped to reinforce the church's purpose statement: "We want to see unbelieving people become the committed followers of Jesus Christ."[1]

The apostle Peter had the same commitment. He encouraged his audience to live good lives that are distinguishable from pagans and that glorify God (v. 12). This principle is applied in several ways: first, within family life (1 Peter 3:1). Wives are to be wise, and the inference is that this will have an evangelistic benefit.

Similarly, in 1 Peter 3:15, Peter's hearers and today's hearers alike should be "apt with their answers, so that when people ask about the hope you have, you may be able to explain it in such a way that unbelieving people might become [Christ's] followers." When we take this to heart, we will make the good news central to all that we have.

Alistair uses specific examples of what this might mean in practice for congregation members: prayers will be focused on God's agenda to see nonbelievers become believers; money will be set aside for this task, with one million dollars of their budget being used expressly for worldwide evangelism; and they will aim to be involved evangelistically in every other area of life: work, resources and everyday conversations.

Alistair then concludes by returning to the main theme of the sermon, namely, that one area that the church might easily overlook is the impact of the gospel through their regular gatherings Sunday by Sunday. "One of the greatest opportunities we have at Parkside is the routine opportunity to 'declare his praises' week by week in corporate worship," he says.

The regular repetition of the simple refrain: "that you may declare [his] praises" (1 Peter 2:9) ensures that, even as Alistair gets into the detail of the biblical text, the congregation is able to keep hold of the central theme.

Apply your own current reading directly into the sermon. Alistair had been inspired by reading two books: *The Priority of Preaching* and *Promoting the Gospel.*[2]

The first book contains advice and encouragement to the ordinary pastor in an ordinary church. For Alistair, it provides a reminder that it is a mistake to be preoccupied with the extraordinary, for most of life is ordinary. God is a God of the ordinary; he puts his treasures in old clay pots.

The second book urges the local church to use its privilege in order to proclaim the gospel creatively. It challenges Alistair to ask specific questions of Parkside, including "Am I and are my colleagues seriously engaged in teaching the Bible?" and "Am I ensuring that the gospel is being proclaimed?"

These books provide specific shape and application for the sermon, leading Alistair to conclude that there is an inherent danger in the way their church is organized. It is easy to develop a mindset which sees everything other than Sunday services as opportunities for the gospel. He says, for example, "We put so much effort into our Christian concerts, which are largely singing, with little opportunity for preaching. If we go to the Bible, we find that it is our Bibles that keep us straight." However, Alistair points out that the gatherings of God's people to praise him do have a significant impact on those who are observing the praise.

These books forced Alistair to ask questions of himself. Having spent some time thinking about them, he was then able to ask the same questions of the congregation and in turn provide insight and direction for them.

Demonstrate how this main point is also made elsewhere in the Bible. The use of cross-references helps build the case that the single theme of the sermon is not an isolated or minor point. Rather, it concurs with what is said elsewhere in the Bible.

In Psalm 96, for example, it is quite evident, Alistair says, that the worshiper "does not go into a closet to declare [God's] praises. Rather, the declaration of God's praise was set within the framework of the surrounding nations. This is not a call to isolation, but a call to engagement. The consequence of this was that declaring the praises of God had an impact. It forced Israel's neighbors to ask, 'Why did they say that? Why did they do that? Do they believe that Yahweh is the only God?' "

This is also illustrated in Psalm 100. We may picture the gathering of God's people with the surrounding nations looking on at their worship.

Alistair cross-references two other biblical passages (Isaiah 43:21; Romans 15:5) to make his point that the congregation's attitude toward corporate worship matters, not just for the worshiper's sake but also for the impact that it has outside the congregation.

Without straying far from the central thrust of the sermon (from the single verse 1 Peter 2:9), the cross-references help the congregation to see that this is not a tangential theme, unrelated to the big sweep of what is said elsewhere in the Bible.

Point to an external historical event which backs up your point. At the time of the Second Temple, the people of God were encouraged to see their mission to the wider world.[3] The court of the Gentiles, Alistair argues, was not just to exclude them but to provide the means whereby they could get close to the worship of God's people, so that they might become converts of Judaism. He says,

> The historian Josephus speaks of evangelistic Judaism, in which crowds of Greeks were attracted by the strength of the praise. The Jews were expelled [from Rome] in 119 BC and AD 17, both times on account of the fact that too many Roman citizens were converting to Judaism.

This historical background enables today's reader to understand why Peter argues his point in the way he does. Living stones are built together; God's people meet together to declare his praises, and all this has an impact on the wider pagan society.

The external verification of the events of the cross is important for Alistair, as illustrated in a talk he gave on 1 Corinthians 2:1-5 (quoting Graeme Goldsworthy):

Telling people the need for the gospel, both their felt need and the real need, is plainly important, but it is not itself the gospel. . . . Whenever people's sense of assurance of salvation is expressed in the first person, something is amiss. When the question "How do you know God will accept you?" is answered by "I have Jesus in my heart," "I asked Jesus into my life," "The Holy Spirit is in me," and so on, the real gospel basis for assurance needs to be reviewed. We rejoice when the answer comes in the third person: "God gave his only Son to die on the cross for me," "Jesus died, rose, and is in heaven for me." When the focus is on the finished and perfect work of Christ, rather than on the yet unfinished work of the Spirit in me, the grounds for assurance are in place.[4]

Help the congregation think through your thoughts with you. As I have listened to Alistair's sermons, I have been struck by the way he brings the congregation into his thinking process. Some preachers never do this except in their final conclusive thoughts. But it can be helpful for the congregation to have your "working" and current thinking, showing how you arrived at the points you are making, in order that, in their own reading and application of the Bible, they too may be able to make links for themselves.

Alistair states, for example, "I had thought that 'declare [his] praises' was just another phrase for evangelize, so I went to check." In 1 Peter 1:12, the word "preached the gospel to you" could be translated "evangelizing you." (It is the same verb in verse 1 Peter 1:25 and 4:6.)

But the word "declare his praises" is *exanggello* [1 Peter

2:9]; a liturgical word. It alludes to something that took place in the context of the corporate gatherings of God's people. It is commonly used in the Septuagint (the Greek translation of the Old Testament), in the Psalms. When the people of God gather, pray, read the Bible, rehearse the creeds, proclaim the Scriptures, sing psalms and spiritual songs, then they are declaring the praises of him who called them out of darkness into his marvellous light.[5]

He brings the congregation to the conclusion that he himself reached: "Here's the burden that I feel: to pray, to plan, to participate in our routine Sunday services in such a way that our corporate worship, our gathered praise, is at least these three things: gospel-focused, heartfelt, intelligible."

Use measured and exact language with passion backed up by demonstration. Alistair asks what happens when we meet to "declare God's praises" on a Sunday? Because there are visitors present, people are eavesdropping on the worship; they are beginning to learn. There is something vastly different about our religious exercises. As a result of this, visitors are forced to say, "I don't know what's going on here." And people will "read" a person's life long before they read any book about the Christian faith. Alistair makes some interesting points:

> Listen carefully: this is why what you do matters. It matters when you show up . . . if you turn up late you are making an impact . . . because you are here to declare the praises of him. . . . People take us and read us. . . . Paying attention to what happens here matters. . . . The volume of our singing matters; the preparation of our hearts matters.

It all matters because of what it is about: it is about declaring his praises.

There is a specific and direct challenge to the congregation. Alistair applies this message first to himself, but then to them:

This is not rhetoric. I have no doubt that I can improve in what I do. But here's the deal: so can you! You can improve equally as much as me. What I want to lay on you is a challenge to set before us: that we dare not neglect what we have in the pursuit of what we might wish we might have. It is to this task we pledge ourselves so that we might declare the praises of him . . .

Gather the disparate parts of the message into a coherent conclusion. The message of 1 Peter 2:9 is succinctly summarized as a threefold duty and expectation of Sunday worship. It should be gospel-focused, heartfelt and intelligible. Having made a number of subpoints throughout the sermon, Alistair helps his congregation memorize the specific final implications.

He asks, Do you know the one single reason why evangelical churches grow? It is because people invite their friends. It does not require fancy programs. All you need to say is, "Why don't you find out?" Of course, if you are not inspired or excited, you are not going to be quick to invite others. Alistair quotes John Dickson: "Normal church meetings conducted exceptionally well will not only inspire the regulars but draw in visitors."

Finally, Alistair acknowledges that there may be reasons why the congregation is reluctant to "declare [Christ's] praises" (lack of enthusiasm, selfishness and lack of interest), but he reminds them that the force of this text, and indeed, the whole of the Bible, is that all should be actively engaged in this role.

LESSONS FOR PREACHERS

- Make a single, simple point in your sermon. Ensure that this is evident from the Bible passage. Repeat it, reinforce it, lodge it in people's minds and ensure that when the congregation leaves, they are sure of what it is.

- Ensure that you are reading both contemporary authors and historic books. Credit your sources. Bring the congregation into your thinking and help them to see why you have connected your thinking and reading with the passage you are expounding.

- Make specific and direct application to the congregation, and include yourself in that application. Help the congregation to know exactly what change you anticipate as a result of a better understanding of the text you have expounded.

- Be passionate and don't be afraid to show the congregation that you believe what you are preaching. Include why you are passionate, rather than merely *saying* that you are passionate!

12

MARK DRISCOLL

Teach with Directness, Challenge and Relevance

❖

Mark and Grace Driscoll started Mars Hill Church in the United States in 1996, with a small group of people meeting in their rented Seattle home. They soon ran out of space. By the time the congregation had a thousand members, it had moved into a renovated hardware store in downtown Seattle.

Theirs is a contemporary upbeat church with an emphasis on what some might consider to be old-school Calvinistic preaching. Says Mark:

> Since being founded in 1996, Mars Hill has placed a high value on engaging the culture around us with the gospel of Jesus Christ. Just as the Apostle Paul and others used letters to communicate to Christians scattered around the ancient world, we see the use of modern-day technologies as a continuation of the gospel reaching the ends of the earth.[1]

In recent years there has been some controversy regarding certain aspects of Mark's preaching ministry, and specifically regarding his use of direct and strong language in sermons.

Blog posts, YouTube clips and other writings give a fuller picture of his preaching.[2]

Of course, our strengths are also our weaknesses. The things we do well may also be areas in which we are most likely to trip up. In this chapter I want to focus on the positive aspects of Mark's preaching and look at the way his plain speaking and directness can be used to good effect. I won't give a full critique of everything that Mark says, but rather focus on those things in preaching he does well.

Mark is a straight-talking preacher, reaching people in a part of the United States which is not known for its high church attendance and which other churches often do not reach. He moves easily between explanation of the biblical text and application to contemporary life, which makes his sermons easy to listen to and immediately applicable.

WHAT MAKES MARK DRISCOLL
A GOOD COMMUNICATOR?

I'm focusing mainly on two sermons preached a year apart. The first is on 2 Corinthians 3:7–4:6 and titled "It's All About Jesus: Glory,"[3] and the second on Luke 9:51-62 and titled "Jesus Before All."[4]

Speak freely and with few notes. One of the striking things about Mark's preaching is that he is more or less free from notes. I think that this is due to his having a good memory and reading widely, and using his conversational and engaging style to refocus the sermon continually on his main preaching theme. He is good at "thinking on his feet," and on some occasions has even had congregation members texting questions which he will answer from the front.

When comparing the notes different preachers use, Josh Harris records Mark Driscoll as saying that he uses very few. He sticks Post-it notes with scribbled comments to the side of his Bible, and uses stories and illustrations that come to him as he preaches.[5] However, he reads a lot and spends much time thinking through not only the content but also the structure of the sermon, something that is obvious from what follows.

Mark's largely unscripted and conversational sermons are long (often over an hour)—not many people can preach like this. But here is a challenge for any preacher: Are you familiar enough with your material to be able to speak with few notes and engage the congregation directly?

Define biblical words and context in a way the congregation can relate to. In the sermon on 2 Corinthians 3:7–4:6, Mark defines *glory* as "God is beautiful, precious, preeminent, prominent, great, magnificence, perfection, excellence and excellent nature, captivating, altogether enthralling, jaw-dropping, breathtaking."

This is no abstract theological term, for the biblical understanding of glory is reflected in our human interests. We have an insatiable appetite for that which is glorious, and are drawn to it.

For example, we see this in the glory of a highly trained athlete. By witnessing the spectacle, we get to enjoy it. We go to beautiful places in the world and see something of the glory of God revealed in his creation. At a wedding there is a part known as the unveiling of the bride, where the congregation may behold her glory. "So when the Bible speaks of glory," says Mark, "it means that at the end of history there will be an unveiling of the bride of Christ."

In the sermon on Luke 9:51-62, "Jesus Before All," Mark spends some time explaining the importance of the city of Jerusalem. It is thought that there were about 100,000 people living in Jerusalem in Jesus' day. It is called "The City of God," carved out of rock, and archaeologists have found ten layers of civilization, one upon the other. Mark explains:

It is the place where Abraham nearly sacrificed his son, and now his son carries his wood to his point of death. The temple was built there, foreshadowing Jesus' sacrifice. It is mentioned 800 times in the Bible. Jerusalem is a significant city.

Large chunks of the sermon are devoted to defining words and phrases in order to help the congregation make sense of the broader context of the Bible passage.

Mark goes on to explain that they have reached a hinge position in the Gospel of Luke. Jesus sets his face toward Jerusalem and onto heaven. He is committed to seeing his task through to completion. "If it were a movie, this would be the point of climax where the hero lays it all on the line," says Mark.

This is the transition place, after which Jesus will march toward his conflict in Jerusalem. Mark explains that Jesus is journeying from Galilee in the north to Jerusalem in the south, and as he makes this journey we will see how people respond to different groups, particularly Samaritans. Hence, an appreciation of the place of Jerusalem for the Jew and for the writer Luke is important in order to make sense of the sermon's eventual conclusions.

Use high-quality multimedia presentations which do not distract from the preaching. Mars Hill makes good use of well-produced video and Internet technology. The sermon is interspersed with film of Mark talking from Jerusalem about this biblical passage. The clip gives an extended introduction to the location and history, having been filmed during a trip to the Holy Land several months earlier. Using this clip gives the congregation a clear sense of the geography, size, scope and topography from Galilee in the north to Jerusalem in the south, and Mark notes how the reactions of Samaritans and others to Jesus had much to do with their culture and location. The clip lasts about six minutes.

Give contemporary descriptions of biblical places. Mark metaphorically takes the congregation to ancient Jerusalem and makes them aware of the problems of Samaria in a way that resonates with today's issues. After the video, he shows Jesus' journey from north to south on a map, through Samaria, explaining the historical tension between Jews and Samaritans.

His definition of Samaritans is as follows:

> These were sort of pseudo jack Jews. . . . They had intermarried with pagans, and they established their own temple, their own Bible, their own religion, their own theology, their own pastors. They were just completely cuckoo. This would be like, let's see, Mormon nudist Scientologists. . . . So what would happen is, as God's people journeyed from Galilee to Jerusalem, they would just walk around Utah [instead]. . . . They didn't even know what to do with Samaria. And the hostility between the Jewish people and the Samaritans was intense. Sometimes they would desecrate one another's temple and [there was] a lot of infighting.

Having spelled out the great hostility between the two groups, Mark then explains the shock of Jesus not walking around Samaria but through it, sending people ahead of him.

Jesus has been in small towns with peasants and villagers. He is making his way to Jerusalem, his place of death. "Jesus is rolling with quite a large entourage . . . the Twelve, plus the Seventy, plus many other Facebook friends. . . . And if you're [in] a village of forty or sixty people, you don't have a Ramada Inn . . . a Costco or a Sam's Club."

The disciples go ahead to prepare the way. Jesus is coming, but the Samaritans say they don't want him. They are too wrapped up with their tribe. But even though the Samaritans reject Jesus, he is patient with them. He won't allow James and John to placard "Turn or Burn."

Mark easily slides from descriptions of the topography, religion and customs of two thousand years ago to equivalent circumstances and practices today. He uses irony and sarcasm in his description, and to his critics he has defended the use of this kind of language, citing Jesus' and other New Testament writers' use of similar language.[6]

Help the congregation to keep focused by reminding them of your central point. In Mark's sermon on 2 Corinthians 3:7–4:6, titled "It's All About Jesus: Glory," he regularly reminds his congregation of his main points—identity, communion, mission and worship—which translate into the following headings:

• Jesus' Glory Defines Our Glory

• Jesus' Glory Makes Worship Possible

• Jesus' Glory Creates Our Community

• Jesus' Glory Compels Our Ministry

In his sermon on Luke 9:51-62, titled "Jesus Before All," Mark concludes by recounting Jesus' conversations with three men who each put something ahead of following Jesus:

- The man who put comfort before Jesus (vv. 57-58)
- The man who placed security above Jesus (vv. 59-60)
- The man who wanted to look back to his past before following Jesus (vv. 61-62)

Nuance application with a sense of urgency, but without condemnation. The conversations with the three men follow after the Samaritans reject Jesus. This leads Mark to make the following points of application:

1. In the case of the man who put comfort before Jesus, the congregation needs to know that following Jesus is the best life, but it certainly is not the easiest. "I'd rather be broke, sick and sad with Jesus. You're following a broke, homeless guy who got betrayed and murdered," says Mark.

2. In the case of the man who placed security above Jesus, he discourages the congregation from making following Jesus our second priority. Do not say, "I want to follow you, but first . . ." How about you? "I will follow Jesus: once I am out of college/ once Im married/once I've paid off my college debt." People continue to push following Jesus out into a future life stage. The "someday" needs to be today.

3. In the case of the man who wanted to look back to his past before following Jesus, Mark warns: "Jesus knows that if this man goes back, he will never go forward. No, don't go back. You'll never go forward."

Mark extends the plowing analogy Jesus used. The person who plows can only make a straight furrow if he looks forward and not backward. Jesus doesn't look back, but forward to the cross. "You can't plow a straight row if you look back. It is analogous to trying to drive home while looking over your shoulder. Jesus shared a timeless principle: I can't go straight and forward while looking back."

Tell human stories of your own contact with people. Mark makes the point that by saying, "Let the dead bury their own dead" (Luke 9:60), Jesus was not trying to isolate the man from his family, as cult leaders often do. He spends five minutes illustrating this by sharing about a woman in danger of being drawn into a cultlike relationship with a self-proclaimed spiritual leader, and about seeking to persuade her against it, relating several of his conversations with her.

He also speaks about a husband who said he would follow Jesus when he had built up his business. However, he pursued success in his career and ended up leaving his family, reneging on his basic promised commitments.

He describes a third encounter with a girl who said that she would follow Jesus if she could go back to talk it through with her live-in boyfriend. Mark strongly urged her not to go home and have that conversation but to leave him and make a decision there, and then not to look back.

It is striking that, in a congregation the size of Mars Hill, he had had these conversations with individual members.

Conclude in a way that applies the points of the sermon directly. The application of this sermon was direct, personal and simple. There were only two options for the Samaritans in Jesus' day, and there are two for us in our day too: repent or reject Jesus.

The Samaritans were a tribe, and by being wrapped up in their tribe they were unable to follow Jesus. They were willing to have

Jesus, if he endorsed them. Mark asks, "What is your tribe?" Some of us say, I like Jesus and want to follow him, so long as he supports what I already believe. Religions try to have a place for Jesus on their team. But Jesus is God: we follow him; he doesn't follow us. I'm fine with Jesus, we say, so long as he doesn't act like God.

We don't know how the three men in the story responded to Jesus' challenge. Did they choose their tribe, their comfort or their past? Luke "leaves it hanging for you and me to make our own conclusion."

Mark's final illustration was a very personal one:

> I want to share with you why I'm really filled with joy today. . . . I woke up . . . overwhelmed by the fruitfulness that surrounds me. . . . For me, twenty years ago, that day came when I realized, "I belong to Jesus now. . . . I'm going to pray, I'm going to repent of sin." . . . By the grace of God, I've never looked back. . . . There's never been a day that [I] have . . . been perfect in that. . . . But there's a harvest. There's fruitfulness. . . . And in the kindness of God, I get to preach this sermon. . . . It was eighteen years ago today that I married Gracie. . . . It was fourteen years ago that Mars Hill Church started. . . . It's been okay, eyes forward, hands on the plow. . . . Life with Jesus is not the easiest, but it is the best.

The close of the sermon was deeply personal. But it was also very closely tied in to the conclusion of the passage and left the hearer with the realization that this sermon had affected Mark deeply too as he had prepared and reflected on his message.

LESSONS FOR PREACHERS

- Use language that will wake your congregation up. Communicate the message with contemporary vocabulary and with punch and force.

- Preach in a way that you are comfortable with. "Find your own voice," say the homileticians. That's to say, don't preach like Mark Driscoll (or indeed like any of the other preachers in this book), for all preachers need to work out their relationship with their preparation and their notes. Having said this, it is clearly evident that Mark can preach without notes, because he reads widely and works hard to memorize information and sermon structure. All preachers should do this!

- Provide the background information that the congregation needs in order to understand the Bible passage. This should be done in an engaging way, helping the congregation to see the parallels between life today and life in the Bible setting.

- Be a people person. Sermons will not engage if you are not having conversations and building relationships with congregation members and non-Christians. Be careful how you relate stories of your encounters with others (and always respect confidentiality), but include them in your sermons so that people can see that you are consistent in what you say in the pulpit and how you relate to people during the rest of the week.

13

MARK DEVER

Expose All of God's Word to All of God's People

❖

Mark Dever is the senior pastor of Capitol Hill Baptist Church in Washington D.C. He and his wife, Connie, share ministry together in Washington. They are parents to two adult children.

One of the striking features of Mark's regular preaching is the meaty substance and the length of sermons, for most last a little over one hour and contain few anecdotes and witticisms—in contrast to those of many contemporary and popular preachers.[1] Sermons are gimmick free and offer little comment on contemporary issues. In preparing a sermon series, Mark comments that he does not seek to be topical or to address directly what he perceives to be current needs. His goal is to let the systematic preaching of the Bible set the agenda for the message. Consequently, his concern is to preach through the whole of the Bible in a coherent and organized way.

Mark's book *9 Marks of a Healthy Church* contains relatively unedited transcripts of sermons preached at Capitol Hill Church, and thus it succeeds in enabling the reader to "hear"

Mark's preaching. He argues that "expositional preaching made all the Bible's teaching on the church more central to me, and for that reason it is the central means of building up the congregation."[2]

The importance of what he calls "expositional preaching" is not only the first of the "nine marks," but very much at the heart of life at Capitol Hill Church. Says Mark,

> We will die without God's Word. Expositional preaching . . . is exposing God's Word to God's people. An expositional sermon takes the main point of a passage of Scripture, makes it the main point of the sermon, and applies it to life today.[3]

The book then goes on to argue that "expositional preaching" is modeled in the Bible. It is necessary because it is through speaking that God accomplishes what he wants to accomplish (see Genesis 1:3; Isaiah 55:10-11; Acts 12:24). And for sermons to be accompanied with God's power, preachers must preach what God says.

Examples of this kind of preaching and teaching could be observed when Levitical priests taught the law (Deuteronomy 33:10), when Ezra and the Levites read from the law and explained it (Nehemiah 8:8), and when Peter and the apostles expounded Scripture, urging their hearers to respond with repentance and faith (Acts 2:14-41; 13:16-47). This is in contrast with those who "speak visions from their own minds, not from the mouth of the LORD" (Jeremiah 23:16, 18, 21-22), and who receive God's condemnation.

Expositional preaching aims to make God's (not the preacher's) agenda the controlling one for church. Thus it is that God's Word, and not the preacher's words, convicts, converts, builds up and sanctifies God's people (Hebrews 4:12; 1 Peter 1:23; 1 Thessalonians 2:13; John 17:17). This kind of preaching exposes God's Word to the congregation.

WHAT MAKES MARK DEVER A GOOD COMMUNICATOR?

Develop the art of synthesis. In the sermon on biblical theology Mark succeeds in summarizing the whole sweep of the biblical story in fewer than a thousand words. Indeed, the entire sermon on this topic is summed up in the following memorable sentence:

> We can summarize the main storyline of the Bible simply in under five words: this is what the Bible teaches us about God: that He is creating; that He is holy; that He is faithful; that He is loving; and that He is sovereign.[4]

Even though this sermon covers this broad sweep of biblical history, the congregation can easily retain five words about God: *creating, holy, faithful, loving* and *sovereign*, as a memorable synthesis. This observation is reminiscent of David Cook's comments made to students at Wycliffe Hall: "The gifts required for preaching include the art of summary. Sermon preparation starts with a summary in your own words. This is not an interpretation of the passage but a summary of the content."[5]

Take time to establish the relevance and significance of your subject matter. Mark Dever takes between five and ten minutes to introduce his sermon "Jesus Cursed," from Mark 11:20-26.[6] The lengthy introduction is a significant feature of his preaching, and on this occasion it took place even before the reading of the Bible passage.

Mark first outlines the problem of making money in the name of religion: preaching that boldly proclaims that God wants us to be healthy and wealthy in this life. Joyce Meyer, Kenneth Copeland and Benny Hinn are examples he gives of those who propagate this false teaching.

Second, Mark identifies the personal anguish which many in the congregation feel when praying for a loved one while being uncertain of the answers to their prayers. Because of abuses, he argues, this biblical text (Mark 11:20-26) has been a bit of an embarrassment to Christians. "The Bible isn't like a promise box or a Ouija board," he says.

The sermon introduction combines the personal anxiety his hearers experience relating to unanswered prayer with general problems and confusion relating to false prosperity preaching on television. These two scenarios lead Mark to the text: "Therefore I tell you, whatever you ask for in prayer, believe that you have received it, and it will be yours" (Mark 11:24).

Specifically apply the sermon to the range of people present. A striking feature of Mark's sermons is the way that he makes very direct application to specific groups in the congregation. This he does at the end of each substantial point, helping the hearers make a direct link to their lives.

Notice these phrases and sentences: "Those who are new to us today . . ."; "Friend, if you are here today and you're not a Christian . . ."; "Let me tell you that as one who used to be an agnostic . . ."; and "My Christian friends, if you want to apply this, you too need to understand . . ." Likewise, "My friend, is that you? Will you trust in [God's] will today?"; "His Spirit will come and live in you today, if only you will turn from your self-run life and trust him"; and "If you're here this morning as a

Christian, consider that we have to know something of God's purposes and revealed will if we are to trust him as we should."

Let's look at this more specifically.

Mark addresses practical concerns relating to being in God's will. How can I do God's will if I don't *know* God's will? Have you considered Christ's will for your life? And think what it means that Christ is the One who has power to deliver on all God's promises. Mark says,

> Some here may think they know God's will and they don't like it. His plan seems plain or too painful. I beg you to see that for what it is; it is pride and arrogance, the thought that you can run God's world better than he can himself. We are identified as his people as we believe his promises. . . . This is only for those who believe in Christ. He hasn't told us everything; he has told us enough and more than enough. Here in his Word his will is revealed.

He acknowledges real anxieties and problems. "In a group this size," Mark says, "if we amounted all the problems which we are dealing with—fear, loss, aimlessness, joblessness . . . God tells us all we need to know in order to pray. This mountain of troubles he is able to sink in the ocean of his love."

And to new Christians he explains that we pray, "in Jesus' name," because we "think that this prayer is consistent with God's revealed will."

Mark offers specific help for praying. He says,

> My Christian friend, [following Jesus' pattern of prayer] is why we pray as we do; [see] for example Mark 14:36, where Jesus too prays [in] this way. Friend, if you're not a Christian today, these are sweet words. God offers [that we]

give up our grudges and realize that he will care for truth and justice. Ask God for forgiveness for yourself, and you might be surprised by how the shackles of hatred fall off.

This type of application is quite explicit and direct. Many preachers fall into the trap of ending their sermon with a general expression such as: "And may God help us to apply this to our lives today." The preceding examples show that a sermon should be applied much more specifically and directly than it often is, so that the congregation is not left wondering how to make personal and specific sense of the sermon in their own lives.

Pay careful attention to the detail of the biblical text. Mark asks questions that take him into the complexities of the passage, and he allows the congregation to think through the answers with him.

His sermon poses four questions They are simple and memorable, and also quite general. But the questions lead the hearer directly into the Bible passage, in anticipation of the answer.

1. Who is Jesus? This question arises from a reading of Mark 11:20-22. The preacher's point here is that Jesus is our example. He models an attitude and a confidence in prayer which his disciples are to emulate. He reminds the congregation that according to Luke's timeline Jesus cleansed the temple and cursed the fig tree on the Monday. Jesus' teaching in Mark 11 takes place on the Tuesday.

Having stayed in Bethany for the night, Jesus and the disciples are now walking back into Jerusalem, and the disciples notice that the cursed tree is completely dead. Peter remembers Jesus' curse and seems surprised at this miracle. What becomes evident in Mark 11 is that Jesus had a purpose in cursing the tree. This gives us a vivid illustration of the fate of Jerusalem (Mark 13:2). Jesus' purpose was to show us how we should relate to him, and so "Who is Jesus?" is a very good question to ask.

2. *Who is Jesus talking to?* Verse 22 is an exhortation to God's people. "Friends, it is crucial that we have confidence in God's complete goodness and unerring wisdom and his unlimited power," says Mark. "How else will we approach him in confidence?"

Jesus assured the people that they should "go head first" into God, trusting his promises. He teaches this again and again (v. 23). And to trust God in his power, we have to trust God and his purposes. "God's power can never be used for anything other than God's purposes," he says (v. 24).

Mark encourages the congregation to be thankful to God for his amazing answers to prayer. And we should be increasingly *expectant* that God will answer our prayers.

3. *What is prayer?* This passage shows that prayer is more than just asking. It includes this, but prayer is also communicating with God. The acronym ACTS illustrates this: Adoration, Confession, Thanksgiving and Supplication.

Mark's sermon addresses directly the seemingly outlandish claim that through prayer we will "move mountains" (v. 23). Passages such as Zechariah 14 teach that things that are impossible with humans are possible with God. Understanding the scope of the Bible's teaching on prayer enables us to understand Jesus' words as a metaphor for "doing the impossible." Hyperbole is common in any language. Using the vivid language of love, we may sing words like "Anything you want," a further example of such hyperbolic vocabulary.

Jesus is not teaching his disciples to be magicians, but he *is* teaching them to do those things that will bring God glory. The "whatever" of verse 24 is shaped by the controlling desire for God to be glorified. Mark says,

> What are those mountains which you will pray for God to move? Some man you've been praying for in your office? A child? Husband? Wife? The salvation of a loved one? Health? Submit them all to God's own glory. Pray that you will see God glorified in everything, exceeding the desire for anything else.

4. What does faith look like? The surprise of verse 25 is that true faith shows itself in forgiveness. Christians know forgiveness from God and therefore forgive others. Without forgiving others, we bring into question God's forgiveness of us. Says Mark,

> When I treated Jesus as I did and contrast that with how he has treated me, this gives me a model for how I should treat you. Forgiving others is evidence that God has forgiven you. How much of your gossip is filled with grudges about what others have done wrong? There should be a deliberate pattern of laying down our grudges.

The subsequent destruction of the temple should not make us conclude that God is no longer able to hear our prayers. Rather, the holy place is being replaced by a truly holy people. Says Mark, "For successful prayer we need faith and forgiveness. The summit is God's forgiveness of us, which can come only through the gift of God in Christ. God calls us to work for those things for which we need his power."

One of the remarkable things about Mark's style of preaching is the way he asks questions that at first glance seem unrelated to the passage. For example, I did not immediately think that Who is Jesus? is the kind of question that I, for one, would have asked of this passage. However, the question becomes immediately relevant when Mark sets it in the broader context of Jesus' cursing of the fig tree and cleansing of the temple. Jesus' right to act as he did is very much tied in with: Who is Jesus? Combining simple and deeply relevant questions and engagement with the passage enables us to make connections with what has contemporary relevance.

Engagement means allowing both yourself and the text to interact with individuals as you prepare. Mark's intense engagement with the text might give the mistaken impression that his preaching is heavy or somber. Colleague Greg Gilbert has written the following about watching Mark Dever prepare his sermons:

> "Hmmm, [says Mark,] I think I'll take as my text for this Sunday . . . the Old Testament." And then he does it, and paints a picture of God's work of redemption that is nothing short of stunning.
>
> I've sat across Dever's desk from him many times when he's [been] preparing his sermons. He doesn't need quiet. No, strike that—he doesn't like quiet. He wants people coming in and out of his study all day when he's working, and on warm days he even sits out in his yard with his laptop so he can talk to people when they walk by. At the end of it all, he has a manuscript that sometimes runs to 12 or 13 pages—not every word he's going to say, but close. He underlines the first word of every sentence in the manuscript so he can look down easily and find his place.[7]

We have noted the importance of human interaction, during and alongside sermon preparation in the case of David Cook's and Mark Driscoll's preaching. But what is striking about Mark Dever is the way that he seems *actively* to desire human contact during the process of preparation in order to help him see how the sermon relates to life. This is in sharp contrast to the rather scholastic model of sermon preparation which many frown upon, whereby the preacher retreats into his study with his books and emerges some time later with a sermon script. We will return to this in the conclusion.

Don't fake emotion, but if you feel it, show it. Mark's careful and methodical approach to the text is balanced by the passion he feels for his subject matter. When reading quotes from John Bunyan's *Pilgrim's Progress* (in a sermon on 1 Corinthians 15:19), he is clearly moved by the reality of heaven, and struggles to stifle his emotion. The key point here is that it seems to be the content of the teaching that moves Mark, rather an inherent character trait.

Summarize your key points. At the end of each section on the sermon on Mark 11, Mark summarizes the point in a sentence that applies directly to the congregation:

• Pray that God will give us faithful preachers of his Word.

• We are God's people, those who trust him.

• God's people share God's purposes and receive God's power.

• For successful prayer, we need faith and forgiveness.

At the end Mark acknowledges that unanswered prayer is a real issue for him as well as for everyone else. Nevertheless, he concludes with five practical observations about prayer which should encourage the congregation to persist:

- Don't mistake not-yets as nevers.

- As you grow in your knowledge of God's purposes, grow too in boldness in your praying.

- Our good God doesn't answer all our prayers in the way we ask them, and thank God he doesn't. (What if all your prayers had been answered in the way you had prayed them?) We are not the wisest of masters, even for ourselves.

- The day is coming when all our prayers will be answered (see Isaiah 65). When we see God, we shall be like him, and all our desires will be met in him.

- Our most important prayer has always been answered: namely, for God to be glorified in saving us in Christ. Jesus was cursed for us. Faith in Christ removes the mountain, casting it into the depths of the ocean, never to threaten us again.

Thus, the specific points of Mark 11 are concluded with some general points of application about prayer.

LESSONS FOR PREACHERS

- Apply the sermon to the variety of people in the congregation, such as the mature Christian, the new Christian, the non-Christian and the doubter.

- Take time to ensure that the congregation understand the specific questions being addressed by the sermon. Help them to see the relevance for their life and witness today.

- Let the shape and flow of the biblical text direct and control your sermon. It is worth asking yourself: Does the congregation come away with a strong sense that God's Word has taken root in their hearts and minds? Has the sermon structure been hidden behind the central message of this passage of Scripture?

- When you prepare your sermon, don't be tempted to retreat from real life, but engage with real people!

CONCLUSION

Preaching That Changes Lives

But as for you, continue in what you have learned and have become convinced of, because you know those from whom you learned it, and how from infancy you have known the holy Scriptures, which are able to make you wise for salvation through faith in Christ Jesus. All Scripture is God-breathed and is useful for teaching, rebuking, correcting and training in righteousness, so that the man of God may be thoroughly equipped for every good work.

In the presence of God and of Christ Jesus, who will judge the living and the dead, and in view of his appearing and his kingdom, I give you this charge: Preach the Word; be prepared in season and out of season; correct, rebuke and encourage—with great patience and careful instruction. For the time will come when men will not put up with sound doctrine. Instead, to suit their own desires, they will gather around them a great number of teachers to say what their itching ears want to hear. They will turn their ears away from the truth and turn aside to myths.

But you, keep your head in all situations, endure hardship, do the work of an evangelist, discharge all the duties of your ministry. (2 Timothy 3:14–4:5)

We return to a passage quoted at the beginning of this book, because it is essential to hold Paul's vision for biblical preaching alongside that of Jesus and those other preachers we have met.

This 2 Timothy passage teaches us a number of key things about good preaching. These verses build in intensity, climaxing in the critical preaching ministry which Timothy is to fulfill.

- Timothy should continue in the faith he learned and has become convinced of, being thankful for that which his grandmother and mother taught him (2 Timothy 3:15; see also 2 Timothy 1:5).

- Timothy should persist in the faith by continuing in Paul's teaching, but appreciate that suffering and godliness go hand in hand (2 Timothy 3:12-13). This will equip him to endure and pass on the message to a second and third generation beyond the apostle Paul (2 Timothy 2:2).

- Timothy should value the Bible. It is God's appointed means to bring us to new life and faith, and the means whereby we are equipped for all God's work (2 Timothy 3:16-17).

- Timothy should hear the weighty charge to be a preacher, which brings with it a huge sense of accountability before God (2 Timothy 4:1).

- Timothy should fulfill this ministry, irrespective of the results or reception he receives. Preaching involves correcting, rebuking and instructing. It is the practical means whereby the equipping work of the Bible comes to the ears and lives of hearers (2 Timothy 4:2).

- Timothy should not be distracted by the success of other preachers who hear the call, not of God, but of the audience, and speak messages which soothe and titillate (2 Timothy 4:3-4).

- Timothy should commit himself soberly to the discipline and hard work of preaching, with the prime aim of explaining the gospel of salvation to his hearers (2 Timothy 4:5).

- Turning Timothy into a preacher of Pauline succession (2 Timothy 2:2) requires a combination of faithful ingesting of God's Word over years, prayer and the cultivating of the gifts God has given him (see also 2 Timothy 1:6), utter conviction about the power of the Word of God to transform his life and fortify him to stand by it, diligence in heeding and applying this Word to himself and to his audience, and boldness to preach it faithfully, irrespective of the results.

- We have seen many of these characteristics displayed in our dozen modern-day preachers.

A COMPOSITE PICTURE OF A GOOD PREACHER

The twelve things good preachers do well could be summarized like this:

- Be aware of cultural and philosophical challenges to the gospel.
- Inspire a passion for the glory of God.
- Let the Bible speak with simplicity and freshness.
- Be a Word-and-Spirit preacher.
- Use humor and story to connect and engage, and dismantle barriers.
- Create interest; apply well.

- Preach with spiritual formation in mind.
- Make much of Jesus Christ.
- Preach with urgency and evangelistic zeal.
- Persuade people by passionate argument from the Bible.
- Teach with directness, challenge and relevance.
- Preach all of the Bible to all of God's people.

If we add to this Jesus' authoritative sermons and Paul's passionate plea for faithful preaching, we can say that to be a good preacher requires that you

1. Be relevant and interesting, showing how the Bible applies to life today. Immerse yourself in God's Word so that you are speaking from his and not your own agenda. Also help people to appreciate that God's agenda is controlling what you are saying.

2. Feed your congregation with the Word, but also encourage an appetite for more. Work hard to make your sermon clear, simple and memorable, using repetition, alliteration and rhetorical techniques that work for you. Use language and words as the well-sharpened tools of your trade. Communicate the importance and urgency of what you are saying, allowing it to move both you and your congregation.

3. Use humor and story to reveal your humanity. And be careful to do this in a way that helps the congregation to see that you have found your joy, purpose and meaning in God.

4. Speak naturally and personally. Reveal the ways in which the message has had an impact on you individually. Don't be bookish, but be people-ish! Don't disconnect with people in order to prepare a sermon, but rather prepare by loving, praying for and rubbing shoulders with those people to whom you are preaching.

I have said almost nothing so far about prayer, and very little about the godliness and the integrated life of the preacher, concentrating instead on the act of preaching itself.[1] But in fact none of these points will accomplish anything at all in preaching if the preacher is not himself growing as a Christian and deeply committed to preaching as a spiritual task.

But with these deliberate omissions in mind, let's ask the following questions.

WHEREIN LIES THE POWER OF GOOD PREACHING?

Commenting on Malachi 2:7: "the lips of a priest ought to preserve knowledge," Martin Luther claimed:

> The Word is the channel through which the Holy Spirit is given. This is a [Bible] passage against those who hold the spoken Word in contempt. The lips are the public reservoirs of the church. In them alone is kept the Word of God. You see, unless the Word is preached publicly, it slips away. The more it is preached, the more firmly it is retained. Reading it is not as profitable as hearing it, for the live voice teaches, exhorts, defends, and resists the spirit of error. Satan does not care a hoot for the written Word of God, but he flees at the speaking of the Word.[2]

Many have noted the contrast between Martin Luther, whose passion for the Christian life was well known to others around him, and John Calvin. Calvin was a quiet and less robust man. He said little about his inner life; he was content to walk with God privately, and trace the workings of the Lord in his life.[3] Like all the men recorded in this book, they each had very different styles and approaches to preaching.

You could say that for Calvin the "real presence" of God was not in the Lord's Supper but in the preached Word. This was where God was living and active among his people, and the place where revival and reformation happened.

But this still raises the question: Where does the power reside?

For some the power resides in "the Word." It is certainly true that the Greek word *dynamis* refers to the preached gospel as God's power. Paul explicitly affirms this: "I am not ashamed of the gospel, because it is the power of God for the salvation of everyone who believes: first for the Jew, then for the Gentile" (Romans 1:16).

But does that settle the matter? The German theologian Karl Barth had such a high view of God's free, unfettered sovereignty that he was anxious that we should not so describe the Bible as the Word of God that it restricted God's freedom to speak and act in whatever way he chose.

He felt that to identify Scripture so much with the Word of God risked compromising the supremacy of Christ. The Word of God is God himself; he is the subject and the Lord over the Bible. And, as far as Barth was concerned, to identify Scripture with the Word of God was close to blasphemy. The Word of God is the *Logos*, the second person of the Trinity.[4]

For Barth the Scriptures are to be seen as a *witness* to the Word of God rather than the Word of God itself. The Bible thus becomes the Word of God as preaching is heard and taken to heart, but Barth felt that it was misleading to call the Bible the Word of God, at least in the sense that the second person of the Trinity is the Word of God.

Barth had commendable convictions about God's freedom and sovereignty, and was very clear that God was only knowable by his self-revelation. But some evangelical scholars have rightly questioned why Barth does not also think it conceivable that God can use human agency and human language in order to communicate.[5] Surely God is quite free and able to commission human authors to write God's Word in their words without threatening his sovereign freedom.

The Bible affirms that God remains close to his Word; indeed reading and understanding his Word is not purely an intellectual experience, for without the agency of God the Holy Spirit, human eyes and ears will remain blind and deaf. The Second Helvetic Confession states: "The preaching of the Word of God is the Word of God." This is clearly a larger discussion than we require here, but let's conclude with something that all will be likely to agree on: that preaching is more than the mere utterance of the Word of God. The latter addresses the hearts of human beings today, and preaching is clearly the main way in which this will happen.

For others the power resides in the preacher. Phillips Brooks's much-quoted comment that preaching is "communication of truth through personality" reflects the fact that the role of the preacher in the act of preaching cannot be underestimated.[6] One of the things that has become very clear in our twelve preacher profiles is that the humanity and accessibility of the preacher very much affects the preaching and the receptivity of the congregation. However, to narrow the power of preaching solely to the preacher himself risks the dangers of the celebrity culture, personality cults and human manipulation.

For others the power resides in the role of God the Holy Spirit. So far we have assumed that the role of the Holy Spirit in enabling the preacher to preach the Bible with pertinent application to contemporary situations is a hallmark of powerful preaching. It is also true that it is the dynamic interplay between Word and Spirit that seems to give preaching its power: preaching is the human voice speaking God's message. It is the "heat and light" spoken of by Jonathan Edwards, and "logic on fire" and "eloquent reason," according to Martyn Lloyd-Jones.[7]

So perhaps we should conclude, in answer to the question, Where does the power reside, that the power of preaching is found in the dynamic interplay of Word, Spirit and the godly preacher. This is the kind of preaching summarized earlier as a powerful, relationally based summons by God through his true and living Word.

THE PREACHER, THE WORD AND THE SPIRIT

The intermarriage of preacher, Word and Spirit is

- found in biblical models of preaching

- illustrated in the great revivals of history

- assumed to be necessary by all those who observe powerful preaching

The intermarriage of preacher, Word and Spirit is found in biblical models of preaching. The first chapter of Ezekiel records what for Ezekiel was to be a shattering experience. It was his thirtieth birthday, the year when he would have expected his formal entry into the priesthood.[8] But, far from being a great preferment, it was an occasion which resulted in him sitting by the banks of the river Kebar feeling deeply distressed for seven days (Ezekiel 3:15).

The cause of his depression was because he was to become a prophet, not a priest, and a prophet charged with the task of delivering a difficult message to boot. Jerusalem had been in sharp decline since its rapid fall to Nebuchadnezzar. In Ezekiel's vision three things came together: the heavens opened, God's word came to him, and God's hand upon him produced an audible, spiritual and physical effect.

God is undeniably present. Ezekiel's spirit is stirred within him, and he hears a message from God, but it is one that will be uncomfortable to preach, being first one of judgment. Christopher Wright comments, "This account is full of hasty, disjointed and ungrammatical language, tumbling along as the words struggle to cope with an overwhelmingly awesome confrontation with the majesty of God."[9]

What Ezekiel finally sees is an "appearance of the likeness of the glory of the LORD," and he hears "the voice of one speaking" (Ezekiel 1:28). He is to be God's spokesman, but he must first preach a negative message (see Ezekiel 2).

We, like the people to whom Ezekiel preached, are a people in exile. Hence, Peter's advice: "Dear friends, I urge you, as aliens and strangers in the world, to abstain from sinful desires, which war against your soul" (1 Peter 2:11).

Ultimately, Ezekiel's preaching will bring a message of hope in a hopeless situation. The evidence of Ezekiel's faithful ministry is found in the words: "They will know that a prophet has been among them" (Ezekiel 2:5). Such godly preaching, though often very uncomfortable and personally challenging, is powerful because what the people hear are not the words of the preacher but the very voice and summons of God.

This is precisely what Paul affirmed in his ministry among the Thessalonian church: "Our gospel came to you not simply with words, but also with power, with the Holy Spirit and with deep conviction" (1 Thessalonians 1:5).

I think that this is partly what the late John Stott had in

mind when he wrote: "Theology is more important than methodology. . . . [T]he essential secret is not mastering certain techniques, but being mastered by certain convictions."[10]

The intermarriage of preacher, Word and Spirit is illustrated in the great revivals of history. There are a number of hallmarks of revivals down through the centuries. These include terror and awe in the congregation, a sense both of God's nearness and yet his mighty power and kingly rule, contrition and mourning over our exile from God, and visions, healing and prayer. The key in all these, though, is the sense of God's presence, not least through the preaching of his Word.

One newspaper wrote of the 1904 Welsh Revival:

> The district is in the grip of an extraordinary spiritual force, which shows no sign of relaxation; the churches are united in a solid phalanx; the prayer meetings are so crowded that the places of worship are inadequate to contain them. Some meetings last eight hours with no cessation in prayer and praise and singing; from the lips of the humblest and lowliest pour forth petition which thrills the whole being and the spell of all earthly things seems to be broken. In the street, in the train, in the home and at work; all this is in hushed reverential tones, the theme of all conversation.[11]

Manifestations, rather like the visions of Ezekiel, often accompany revival but they should not distract. One of the reasons why Jonathan Edwards wrote his book *On Revival* was to give an analysis of the 1740-1742 Great Awakening. What are the distinguishing marks of the work of the Holy Spirit? Not the manifestations in themselves, but rather the hallmarks of repentance and ensuing godly living.

The word that is sometimes used to describe such preaching is *unction*:

> There is sometimes something in preaching that cannot be ascribed either to matter or expression, and it cannot be described by what it is, or from whence it cometh, but with a sweet violence it pierceth into the heart and affections and comes immediately from the Word; but if there be any way to obtain such a thing, it is by the heavenly disposition of the speaker.[12]

The word *unction* captures the extraordinary manner in which God transforms the human words of the preacher in such a way that they come with the full force of God's Word, challenging the spirit and giving the hearer the sense that the living God has personally addressed *me* today. I, for one, long for more of that preaching today. We have already observed hints of it from the preachers in this book.

During the eighteenth-century Wesleyan Revival, a stone-mason called John Nelson, from Yorkshire, came home to discover that his wife had been converted through John Wesley's preaching. He was furious, beating and cursing her, as a result. When he had no more strength to beat her, he reminded her that he was a church member, confirmed and religious.

He was so angry that he took a butcher's knife and went after Wesley, intending to murder him. Eventually he caught up with him at Kensington Common in London. He pushed through the crowd, ready to use the knife. But there was such a spirit of conviction at the meeting that Wesley looked him in the eye and said, "Thou art the man." Nelson fell to the ground, crying, "God be merciful to me a sinner." He was not only converted, but ended up as the first of Wesley's lay preachers.

The evidence of good preaching is found in the change not just in an individual's life but ultimately in the transformation of church and society.

The intermarriage of preacher, Word and Spirit is assumed to be necessary by all those who observe powerful preaching. The following wide range of observations demonstrate this point eloquently.

According to Steven Lawson:

Every season of reformation and every hour of spiritual awakening has been ushered in by a recovery of biblical preaching. . . . A heaven-sent revival will only come when Scripture is enthroned again in the pulpit. There must be the clarion declaration of the Bible, the kind of preaching that gives a clear explanation of a biblical text with compelling application, exhortation, and appeal.[13]

Jeffery Crotts commented:

The preacher must always have the goal of personal transformation in his mind as he studies the text. When God's Word and his Spirit transform the preacher's heart and actions through study, prayer and meditation, then and only then, can the preacher authentically model the transforming work of illumination to his hearers.[14]

C. H. Spurgeon said:

I would rather speak five words out of this book than 50,000 words of the philosophers. If we want revivals, we must revive our reverence for the Word of God. If we want conversions, we must put more of God's Word into our sermons.[15]

A. W. Tozer remarked:

Truth engages the citadel of the human heart and it is not satisfied until it has conquered everything there.[16]

And Robert Murray McCheyne urged:

Speak for eternity. Above all things, cultivate your own spirit. A word spoken by you when your conscience is clear, and your heart full of God's Spirit, is worth ten thousand words spoken in unbelief and sin. . . . Remember that God, and not man, must have the glory. . . . If the veil of the world's machinery were lifted off, how much we would find is done in answer to the prayers of God's children.[17]

TO SUM UP

Has this chapter whetted your appetite to pray to God to raise up more godly preachers and to pray for preachers today? We have seen that there is much true and godly preaching in our world. But none of the modern-day preachers listed in this book is perfect. However, I hope you will have noted the things that each one does well, and, if you are a preacher, realize that these things can be done by you too! None of the twelve things listed is beyond any preacher.

There is only so much that the preacher can do. Without the presence of God the Holy Spirit in the heart of the preacher, his words will vanish into thin air. Or, to put this more positively, God in his great mercy uses frail human beings as instruments of his Word and Spirit, to bring about revival, renewal and restoration in his people by the faithful preaching of his Word. Pray to God that this might happen in our own day and age!

APPENDIX

The Survey and Online Resources

My interest in preaching arises partly out of more than twenty-five years of seeking to improve my own preaching. I have also been involved in training preachers in various parts of the world. More recently, since 2007, I have been tutor in homiletics and hermeneutics at Wycliffe Hall, Oxford, teaching future preachers in the Church of England. Hence, I have a personal as well as an academic interest in understanding what good preachers do well.

In 2009, in order to test my own theories, I undertook a survey in which I asked friends, colleagues and associates to answer two brief questions. It did not claim to be a comprehensive or an exhaustive study. I polled students from Wycliffe Hall and everyone in my e-mail address list. I also posted the survey on my Facebook account and on my blog and website (http://metamorphe.wordpress.com and www.Simon vibert.com).

The result was over 250 responses, roughly 40 percent of which were from full-time theological students.

METHODOLOGY
The request was as follows:

90-second preaching survey

I am doing some research into people's favorite preachers. I am very happy to share the results and analysis which will appear on a new website in due course.

Would you be good enough to answer these two short questions?

1. Who is/are your favorite living preacher/preachers, the ones you enjoy listening to?

2. Can you name what it is that this/those preacher does/preachers do that makes you want to listen?

Quite intentionally I asked people to give me their instinctive reaction to these questions. I conjectured that an immediate response would be more reliable. A more thought through, considered or nuanced response would begin to articulate the respective positives and negatives of certain homiletical styles, but this was not my goal. An intuitive response allowed me to consider what it was that kept people listening, and why it was that some preachers drew a crowd while others did not.

Please see the additional resources at www.schoolofpreaching .org, a website which has a growing number of additional profiles of things that good preachers do well and an article which examines Barack Obama's use of rhetoric in his presidential campaign speeches.

NOTES

Preface

[1]Of course, our first preacher, Jesus Christ, is in a league of his own, not subject to my critique, but nevertheless a critical model from whom all preachers should learn.

Introduction

[1]Please see the appendix for details of the survey, which was undertaken in preparation for the writing of this book.

[2]See also Phillip D. Jensen and Paul Grimmond, *The Archer and the Arrow* (Kingsford, Australia: Matthias Media, 2010), as further example of the good things which today's preachers should be doing.

[3]See, for example, Peter Adam, *Speaking God's Words* (Downers Grove, Ill.: InterVarsity Press, 1996); Christopher Ash, *The Priority of Preaching* (Ross-shire, U.K.: Christian Focus, 2009); John Dickson, *Promoting the Gospel* (Sydney: Aquila Press, 2006); John Chapman, *Setting Hearts on Fire* (Kingsford, Australia: St. Matthias Press, 1999); Greg Haslam, ed., *Preach the Word* (Lancaster, U.K.: Sovereign Books, 2006); Bryan Chapell, *Christ-Centered Preaching* (Grand Rapids: Baker, 1994); Haddon Robinson, *Expository Preaching: Principles and Practice* (Leicester, U.K.: Inter-Varsity Press, 1986); and John Stott, *I Believe in Preaching* (London: Hodder & Stoughton, 1982).

[4]See "School of Preaching," *Wycliffe Hall*, www.schoolofpreaching.org for my observations on the rhetorical shape of Barack Obama's acceptance speech.

Chapter 1: Jesus Christ the Preacher

[1]See Eugene Peterson, *Eat This Book: A Conversation in the Art of Spiritual Reading* (Grand Rapids: Eerdmans, 2006).

[2]D. Patte, *The Gospel According to Matthew. A Structural Commentary on Mat-

thew's Faith (Minneapolis: Fortress, 1987), p. 65.

[3]See Matthew 7:21-23: that is, people will be judged on whether they truly acknowledge his lordship (rather than just saying the right words).

[4]Winston Churchill, quoted in Martin Gilbert, *Churchill: A Life* (Portsmouth, N.H.: Heinemann, 1991), p. 656.

[5]See further on this in George A. Kennedy, *New Testament Interpretation Through Rhetorical Criticism* (Chapel Hill: University of North Carolina Press, 1984), pp. 49f; and Joe Carter and John Coleman, *How to Argue Like Jesus* (Wheaton, Ill.: Crossway, 2009).

[6]Four related techniques include *chreia* (anecdote about a named person); *gnōmē* (sententious analogy); *mythos* (fable or parable); and *diegema* (narrative, historical-mythical episode). See Ian H. Henderson, *Jesus, Rhetoric and Law* (Boston: E. J. Brill, 1996) for an exploration of these features in the Gospels.

[7]Treasures in heaven (Matthew 6:19-24), wise and foolish builders (Matthew 7:24-27) and similar sections all display some of the characteristics of a parable.

[8]On *ethos, logos* and *pathos* see also Kent Hughes, "The Anatomy of Exposition: *Logos, Ethos,* and *Pathos,*" *Southern Baptist Journal of Theology* 3 (1999): 45-46.

[9]The process of arriving at a homiletical theme is helpfully explained in Haddon Robinson, *Expository Preaching: Principles and Practice* (Leicester, U.K.: Inter-Varsity Press, 1986).

Chapter 2: Tim Keller

[1]Tony Carnes, "New York's New Hope," *Christianity Today,* December 1, 2004, www.christianitytoday.com/ct/2004/december/15.32.html.

[2]Richard F. Lovelace, *Dynamics of Spiritual Life: An Evangelical Theology of Renewal* (Downers Grove, Ill.: InterVarsity Press, 1979). The key theme of this book is that Christians tend to reverse justification and sanctification, putting their confidence not in the once-for-all imputation of Christ's righteousness but rather in their perception of their advance in sanctification.

[3]See Timothy Keller, *The Prodigal God* (New York: Dutton Adult, 2008), for more on this theme.

[4]Timothy Keller, *Generous Justice* (New York: Dutton Adult, 2010).

[5]See "Redeemer's History," *Redeemer Presbyterian Church,* www.redeemer.com/about_us/vision_and_values/history.html.

⁶Lisa Miller, "The Smart Shepherd," *Newsweek*, February 9, 2008, www .newsweek.com/2008/02/09/the-smart-shepherd.html

⁷Tim Keller, quoted in Ed Stetzer, "More on Tim Keller and Newsweek," EdStetzer.com, www.edstetzer.com/2008/02/tim_keller_on_evolution_and _ot.html.

⁸Josh Harris, "Tim Keller: Preaching Notes," www.joshharris.com/2008/08/ tim_keller.php.

⁹Preached on May 1, 1994, available at http://download.redeemer.com/rpc-sermons/storesamplesermons/Who_Is_This_Jesus.mp3.

¹⁰Huston Smith, *The World's Religions: Our Great Wisdom Traditions* (New York: HarperOne, 1965, 1991).

¹¹Tim Keller, "Doing Justice," *Resurgence,* www.theresurgence.com/r_r_2006_ session_eight_audio_keller.

¹²This illustration is also used in Timothy Keller, *The Reason for God* (New York: Penguin, 2008).

¹³C. S. Lewis, *Mere Christianity* (New York: Collins, 1952), pp. 54-56.

¹⁴Michael Luo, "Preaching the Word and Quoting the Voice," *New York Times*, February 26, 2006, www.nytimes.com/2006/02/26/nyregion/26 evangelist.html?pagewanted=2.

Chapter 3: John Piper

¹See Chris Sugden, "New Mission to England," *Evangelicals Now*, August 2011, www.e-n.org.uk/p-1310–A-passion-for-Piper.htm.

²"Mission and Vision," *Bethlehem Baptist Church*, www.hopeingod.org/ about-us/who-we-are/mission-vision.

³John Piper, *Future Grace* (Colorado Springs: Multnomah Books, 1995), p. 386.

⁴John Piper, *Desiring God* (Colorado Springs: Multnomah Books, 1996), p. 13.

⁵Ibid., p. 14.

⁶Pascal, quoted in ibid., p. 173.

⁷C. S. Lewis, *Reflections on the Psalms* (London: Fount Paperbacks, 1987), p. 80.

⁸Piper, *Desiring God*, p. 83.

⁹John Piper, *The Supremacy of God in Preaching* (Grand Rapids: Baker, 2004), p. 13.

¹⁰See more on Jonathan Edwards in Piper, *Supremacy of God in Preaching*, pp. 69ff.

¹¹Ibid., p. 23.

[12]John Piper, "The Pastor as Theologian," *DesiringGod.org*, April 15, 1988, www.desiringgod.org/resourcelibrary/biographies/1458_the_pastor_as_theologian.

[13]Jonathan Edwards, *Charity and Its Fruits* (London: Banner of Truth, 1961), p. 13.

[14]Jonathan Edwards, quoted in Piper, *Future Grace*, p. 384.

[15]See further my article "Remembering Jonathan Edwards," *Churchman*, www.churchsociety.org/churchman/documents/Cman_117_4_Vibert.pdf.

[16]"John Piper to Be Streamed," *Mars Hill Church*, February 23, 2010, http://blog.marshillchurch.org/2010/02/23/john-piper-event-to-be-streamed.

[17]John Piper, "Passion for the Supremacy of God, Part 1," *DesiringGod.org*, January 2, 1997, www.desiringgod.org/resource-library/conference-messages/passion-for-the-supremacy-of-god-part-1.

Chapter 4: Vaughan Roberts

[1]Nicky Gumbel followed Sandy Millar as Vicar of Holy Trinity Brompton after completing his curacy there.

[2]Vaughan Roberts, *God's Big Picture* (IVP Books), *God's Big Design* (InterVarsity Press), *Life's Big Questions* (IVP Books) and *Authentic Church* (InterVarsity Press); *Battles Christians Face* (Authentic Media), *Missing the Point?* (Authentic Media), *Distinctives* (Authentic Media), *Turning Points* (Authentic Media) and *True Worship* (Authentic Media).

[3]"Ten Questions for Expositors—Roberts," *Unashamed Workman*, http://unashamedworkman.wordpress.com/2007/05/02/ten-questions-for-expositors-vaughan-roberts.

[4]"Vaughan Roberts," *Slipstream*, www.eauk.org/slipstream/podcast/vaughan-roberts.cfm.

[5]"Ten Questions for Expositors—Roberts."

[6]John Stott, *I Believe in Preaching* (London: Hodder & Stoughton, 1982).

[7]See *The Proclamation Trust* website at www.proctrust.org.uk, and the 9:38 website at www.ninethirtyeight.org.

[8]Vaughan Roberts, "God's Merciful Plan," found under "Sermons," *St. Ebbes*, www.stebbes.org.uk.

[9]This is reminiscent of the fourfold sermon structure set out by Paul Scott Wilson in *The Four Pages of the Sermon: A Guide to Biblical Preaching* (Nashville: Abingdon, 1999), whereby the preacher moves from a problem in the world to the problem in the text, to a solution in the text, and finally returning to a solution in the world.

[10]That is, no one will be privileged in favor or prejudiced against on the basis of rank, gender or religion.

[11]Simeon made 2,536 skeletal outlines of sermons and did not deem a sermon ready to preach until it could be outlined in this way! Simeon's preaching is eloquently summarized by J. I. Packer, "Expository Preaching: Charles Simeon and Ourselves," *Churchman*, 1960, www.churchsociety.org/churchman/documents/CMan_074_2_Packer.pdf.

Chapter 5: Simon Ponsonby

[1]Simon Ponsonby, *God Inside Out* (Eastbourne, U.K.: Kingsway, 2007).

[2]A transcript of a talk given by Simon on "Word and Spirit" may be found at www.wenetwork.co.uk/action-zones/christian-community/news/645-simon-ponsonby-12th-november.html.

[3]Evan Roberts, "Consecrate Yourselves to the Lord," referred to in Kevin Adam, *A Diary of Revival* (Nashville: B&H Publishing, 2004), p. 94.

[4]Tony Sargent, *The Sacred Anointing: The Preaching of Dr Martyn Lloyd-Jones* (London: Hodder & Stoughton, 1994), pp. 28-29.

Chapter 6: J.John

[1]"The communication of truth by personality" originated with Phillips Brooks, *Lectures on Preaching, Delivered Before the Divinity School of Yale College in January and February, 1877* (E. P. Dutton, 1877), p. 5. The full quotation runs: "Preaching is the communication of truth by man to men. It has in it two essential elements, truth and personality."

[2]"An Interview with J.John," *Interview*, winter-spring 2006, www.christianvocations.org/online/cv.nsf/0/3E4635F9E21FE17480256A000060CC47/$file/iView_Feb_2006_web.pdf.

[3] J.John preached "Changing in a Changing World" at St. Andrew's Church, Chorleywood, J.John's home church. It can be purchased at www.philotrust.com/shop/browse/67.

[4]This particular sermon began with a story about Jack Verne, who found a bottle floating on the California coast in 1955 and promising the finder a huge inheritance. He concluded by saying, "You would be fool not to check it out." J.John has told me that he no longer refers to this story because he cannot find verification of the facts. Hence, I have included instead a story which he now uses.

Chapter 7: David Cook

[1]"Centre for Preaching," *SMBC*, www.smbc.com.au/pages/default.asp?pid=34.

[2]David Cook, "A Moving Word," an interview by Peter Hastie, *Australian Presbyterian*, February 2008, www.allianceradio.org/AP/2008/AP2.08.pdf.

[3]David Cook, ed., *How to Speak at Special Events* (Ross-shire, U.K.: Christian Focus, 2007), p. 85.

[4]See "School of Preaching," *Wycliffe Hall*, www.schoolofpreaching.org.

[5]James Dobson, quoted in "Purpose," *Exploring Christianity*, www.christianity.co.nz/purpose4.htm.

[6]Cook, *How to Speak at Special Events*, p. 84.

[7]"Double listening" is explained in John Stott, *I Believe in Preaching* (London: Hodder & Stoughton, 1982), tellingly published under the title *Between Two Worlds* (Eerdmans) in the United States.

Chapter 8: John Ortberg

[1]"Ortberg's Ten Deadly Sins of the Preacher," *Preaching.org*, www.preaching.org/ortbergs-ten-deadly-sins-of-the-preacher.

[2]"Don't Waste a Crisis," *Leadership Journal*, January 31, 2011, cited in www.outofur.com/archives/2011/02/epic_fail_pasto.html#more.

[3]See Eugene Peterson, *Working the Angles: The Shape of Pastoral Integrity* (Grand Rapids: Eerdmans, 1989), and Dallas Willard, "On-line Listening," *Dallas Willard*, www.dwillard.org/resources/On-LineListening.asp.

[4]Easter sermon: John Ortberg, "The World's Greatest Step," awaken.me, April 4, 2010, http://awaken.me/2010/04/worlds-greatest-step-john-ortberg/#more-309. Sermon on redemption: John Ortberg, "a.k.a. 'Redeemer,'" June 7, 2009, http://awaken.me/2009/06/aka-redeemer-john-ortberg/#more-125.

[5]John Calvin, *Institutes of the Christian Religion*, trans. F. L. Battles, ed. J. T. McNeill (Philadelphia: Westminster Press, 1960).

[6]"Don't Waste a Crisis."

Chapter 9: Nicky Gumbel

[1]The course was in fact designed by Charles Marnham when he was curate at HTB in 1977, and adapted by subsequent curates.

[2]Nicky Gumbel, "Nicky Gumbel Interview Transcript," interview by Adam Rutherford, *Guardian.co.uk*, August 28, 2009, www.guardian.co.uk/commentisfree/belief/2009/aug/28/religion-christianity-alpha-gumbel-transcript.

[3]Ibid.

[4]http://archive.htb.org.uk/sunday-talks/vision-sunday.

[5]Rosemary Bennett and Mary Bowers, "Loneliness: The Silent Epidemic Sweeping Through Britain," *Times of London*, December 31, 2009, http://tech.groups.yahoo.com/group/evolutionary-psychology/message/100683.

[6]My booklet *Longing for Paradise* deliberately begins with felt needs and then moves readers on to see their real needs in the gospel of Christ: see Simon Vibert, "Longing for Paradise?" *SimonVibert*, www.simonvibert.com/writing/longingforparadise/index.htm, for an online version.

Chapter 10: Rico Tice

[1]"When Rico Met Roger," *Evangelicals Now*, September 2000, www.e-n.org.uk/1254-When-Rico-met-Roger.htm.

[2]For the Christianity Explored website see www.christianityexplored.org.

[3]Michael Horton, "Reviews," Christianity Explored, www.ceministries.org/ce/reviews.

[4]The seven Jewish brothers and their mother referred to in 2 and 4 Maccabees.

[5]A "bleep test" is a fitness test with multistages, used internationally by sports professionals to estimate an athlete's maximum oxygen uptake, in which bleeps are played at structured intervals.

[6]A transcript of this talk may be found at www.ceministries.org/downloads/ce/Christianity%20Explored%20Paperback%20Sample.pdf.

[7]Rico Tice, "Evangelism," www.youtube.com/watch?v=IbNc8BsoUko.

Chapter 11: Alistair Begg

[1]"What We Believe," Parkside Church, www.parksidechurch.com/about/what-we-believe.

[2]Christopher Ash, *The Priority of Preaching* (Ross-shire, U.K.: Christian Focus, 2009), and John Dickson, *Promoting the Gospel* (Sydney: Aquila Press, 2006).

[3]The Second Temple period is marked from the rebuilding of the temple between 520 and 515 B.C. to its destruction by Rome in A.D. 70.

[4]For Alistair's source, see Graeme Goldsworthy, *Preaching the Whole Bible as Christian Scripture* (Grand Rapids: Eerdmans, 2000), p. 95. The talk was given at Bible by the Beach 2010. For their website see www.biblebythebeach.org.

[5]This and other quotations here are from my transcription of parts of Alistair's sermon, which is now archived at www.truthforlife.org/store/products/cd-individual-messages/declaring-his-praise.

Chapter 12: Mark Driscoll

[1]Mark Driscoll, "I Am New Here," *Mars Hill Church*, www.marshillchurch. org/newhere.

[2]The primary sources are on the Mars Hill website (www.marshillchurch .org). See also YouTube clip segment "How Dare You" (www.youtube.com/ watch?v=ZkaeAkJO0w8); YouTube clip on *The Shack* (www.youtube.com/ watch?v=pK65Jfny70Y); helpful summary of John Piper on Mark Driscoll's use of harsh language (www.sfpulpit.com/2008/09/17/john-piper-mark-driscoll-and-harsh-language); and conversation between Mark Driscoll and John Piper (http://theresurgence.com/2008/09/04/interview-with-john-piper-video). A Google search will reveal many more blog posts and video conversations which reflect the contemporary communication style of Mark Driscoll, and discuss his strengths and weaknesses.

[3]September 13, 2009, and August 23, 2010, http://marshill.com/media/its-all-about-jesus/preview.

[4]See "Jesus Before All," http://marshill.com/media/luke/jesus-before-all.

[5]See Josh Harris, "Preaching Notes: Mark Driscoll," *JoshHarris.com*, www .joshharris.com/2008/09/preaching_notes_mark_driscoll.php.

[6]Nathan Busenitz, "John Piper, Mark Driscoll, and Harsh Language," Pulpit, September 7, 2008, www.sfpulpit.com/2008/09/17/john-piper-mark-driscoll-and-harsh-language

Chapter 13: Mark Dever

[1]A noteworthy exception is Mark Driscoll, who also preaches for about one hour.

[2]Mark Dever, *9 Marks of a Healthy Church* (Wheaton, Ill.: Crossway, 2005), p. 14.

[3]Mark Dever, "What Are the 9 Marks?" 9Marks.org, www.9marks.org/what-are-the-9marks.

[4]Dever, *9 Marks*, p. 60.

[5]Comments made in lectures given during the School of Preaching, June 2010.

[6]This is from a series titled "You Might Be Surprised." I recommended that you read Mark 11:20-26 now.

[7]Josh Harris, "Preaching Notes: Mark Dever," JoshHarris.com, www.josh harris.com/2008/08/mark_dever.php. The website also includes the full text of one of Mark Dever's sermons.

Conclusion

[1]See Greg Scharf, *Prepared to Preach* (Ross-shire, U.K.: Christian Focus, 2005), particularly on the necessity of prayer in preaching.

[2]Jarislav Pelikan and Helmut Lehmann, eds., *Luther's Works: American ed.* (St. Louis: Concordia Publishing House, 1955), 18ff., p. 401.

[3]A. Lindt, "John Calvin," *Eerdmans' Handbook to the History of Christianity* (Grand Rapids: Eerdmans, 1977), p. 380.

[4]Karl Barth, *Church Dogmatics* (London: T & T Clark, 1961), 1:120-21.

[5]E.g., Mark Thompson, *A Clear and Present Word* (Downers Grove, Ill.: IVP Academic, 2006), p. 76.

[6]These remarks were made at a series of lectures on preaching delivered at Yale University in New Haven, Connecticut, in 1877.

[7]Martyn Lloyd-Jones, *Preaching and Preachers* (Grand Rapids: Zondervan, 1971).

[8]Some think that this might refer to the thirtieth year of exile.

[9]Christopher Wright, *The Message of Ezekiel* (Downers Grove, Ill.: InterVarsity Press, 1981), p. 46.

[10]John Stott, *I Believe in Preaching* (London: Hodder & Stoughton, 1982).

[11]See R. B. Jones, "Rent Heavens," *Revival Library*, www.revival-library.org/catalogues/1904ff/jonesrb.html.

[12]Attributed to E. M. Bounds; see *Reformation and Revival*, www.reformationandrevival.org.uk/5.html.

[13]Steven Lawson, "Preach the Word," *TableTalk*, January 2010, www.ligonier.org/learn/articles/preach-word.

[14]Jeffrey Crotts, *Illuminated Preaching: The Holy Spirit's Vital Role in Unveiling His Word, the Bible* (Greenville, S.C.: Day One, 2010), p. 57.

[15]C. H. Spurgeon, quoted in Lawson, "Preach the Word."

[16]A. W. Tozer, *Of God and Men* (Camp Hill, Penn.: Christian Publications, 1960).

[17]Robert Murray McCheyne, *The Life and Remains, Letters, Lectures, and Poems of the Rev. Robert Murray McCheyne*, many editions.